D1029310

SOMETIMES WE DANCE ALONE

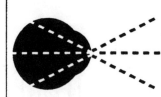

This Large Print Book carries the
Seal of Approval of N.A.V.H.

SOMETIMES WE DANCE ALONE

Your Next Years Can Be Your <u>Best</u> Years!

Edith McCall

G.K. Hall & Co.
Thorndike, Maine

Published in 1995 by arrangement with Brett Books, Inc.

Grateful acknowledgment is made to the following for permission to quote from previously published material:

Outward Bound (Garrison, New York): For permission to quote from its brochures.

University Press of New England (Hanover, New Hampshire): For permission to quote from *The Story of Elderhostel* by Eugene S. Mills. © 1993 by Eugene S. Mills.

G.K. Hall Large Print Inspirational Collection.

The text of this Large Print edition is unabridged.
Other aspects of the book may vary from the original edition.

Set in 16 pt. News Plantin by Rick Gundberg.

Printed in the United States on acid-free paper.

Library of Congress Cataloging in Publication Data

McCall, Edith S.
    Sometimes we dance alone : your next years can be your best years! / by Edith McCall.
      p.   cm.
    Includes bibliographical references.
    ISBN 0-7838-1190-X (lg. print : hc)
    1. Middle-age — United States — Psychological aspects.
2. Middle aged persons — United States — Psychology.
3. Single people — United States — Psychology. 4. Life change events — United States. I. Title.
[HQ1059.5.U5M4 1995]
305.24'4—cd20   94-41433

To the dear people whose lives have
touched mine with love and encouragement.
Because of you, I can
"dance lightly on the edges of time."

CONTENTS

INVITATION TO THE DANCE

Alone Need Never Mean *Lonely*

But the snail replied "Too far, too far!"
    and gave a look askance —
Said he thanked the whiting kindly, but he
    would not join the dance.
Would not, could not, would not, could not,
    would not join the dance.

Lewis Carroll
ALICE'S ADVENTURES
IN WONDERLAND

At some point in our adult years, more and more of us find ourselves living alone and lacking a partner in "the dance of life." Such a situation may have come about by choice or as part of God's plan for us. In either case, most of us have enough talent and energy to do some very lively dancing, mentally if not physically.

Surely, if God has kept us here, it is because He recognizes that we have much of value to contribute to this old world — and much to learn from it. It's time that *we* recognized it too, and approached each new day and year as a precious gift from God. Let's not imitate Lewis Carroll's reluctant snail. Instead, let's open our hearts to the heavenly music and participate in the dance.

Though in the age-65-and-older group women outnumber men by three to one, life expectancy is rising for both sexes. When the twentieth century began, the average life span for a man was only 46 years, and for a woman it was 48. By 1990, after all the wonderful advances in knowledge and treatment of body and mind, life expectancy had risen to 72 for a man and 79 for a woman. And it is still rising! Remember, these are *average* life-span statistics, which include deaths from infancy onward. Today an ever-growing number of people live to 100 or more in good mental and physical health, able to take care of themselves. Aren't we fortunate to be living now instead of at the time of our grandparents?

According to the 1990 United States census reports, 22.7 million people live alone, more than double the 10.9 million recorded in 1970. As we might expect, many of these Americans are in the "September" of their lives, but the percent of younger people choosing to live alone has also increased. Yet, whether it comes to us through destiny or choice, a life alone need never be a life of loneliness.

Among the baby boomers, the custom of making the fortieth birthday a mock-mourning scene has become common. Quite in contrast with that you're-over-the-hill approach was the earlier celebration of that birthday with the saying "Life begins at forty!" I remember that when I reached my fortieth birthday, I received a gift of a baby rattle — a much happier symbol than a black T-shirt with a skeleton on it, representing the departure of the so-called *good* part of life. The "mourning" is supposedly all in fun, but there is a lot more to be said for the life-*begins*-at-forty celebration!

I, married and with two teenage daughters when I reached forty, was one of those who believed that the best was yet to come. But soon afterward, my personal life seemed to be hurtling downhill, and I realized that I was going in the wrong direction. Feeling frustrated and lost along the way, I no longer liked the person I was becoming. With God's help, I redesigned my life. When I was fifty-one, I chose to begin living alone, to dance to my own piper. As I write this, I'm forty the second time around and life is still a lively dance, with only occasional intervals when the music slows to a languorous beat.

Some people, as they reach the age of retirement, overdo the retiring and withdraw from active life because they think they are too old to find new occupations with which to fill their days. They choose to be the occupants of the chairs along the wall in life's ballroom, the wallflowers sitting out the rest of the opportunities for adventure that offer themselves. Even worse, they

11

may choose to avoid the ballroom altogether and become couch potatoes who let the bland gravy of TV sitcoms pour over them day after day. A deadening choice — time then for the mourning party!

There are still some who, upon reaching the seventies milepost, meekly accept the idea from Grandpa's time that living beyond the traditional three score and ten years means inevitable disability. To hold to that belief is to *invite* physical and mental retrogression. The only satisfaction for those in that thinking pattern may be in proving themselves right!

We have a choice — many choices. We may choose to muse on our increasing aches and pains. If that is our choice, it is likely that our talk becomes an "organ recital," and we become bores, even to ourselves. Our bodies, in tune with our minds, become sluggish and begin to break down. The passing years are more endured than lived. When the TV commercials proclaim the start of the flu and cold season, let's push the mute button and turn off those negative forecasts. Those who believe the advertisements had better stock up on tissues and cold remedies!

We choose our own rhythms — to urge us on to our feet or to lull us into nonparticipation in the dance of life. What beat shall we choose to dance to — a polka? swing? fox-trot? waltz? Have we wound down to a stately old minuet, or — heaven help us — a dirge?

Or perhaps we have chosen to turn off the

music entirely because "fate" has left us without a partner. So then, when someone offers us an opportunity to break that pattern, possibly suggesting a voyage, a day trip, a class, a hobby — any activity that would make us venture beyond our familiar routine — fear of the unknown and untried makes us dwell on the worst possibilities. "Oh, no!" we say. "I'd be afraid to do that!" And we end up continuing in our old, tiresome rut.

Or we could be enthusiastic about what is to come, like the woman traveling alone on a cruise ship who heard Big Band music drifting through a closed door at the far end of the corridor. Thinking herself unobserved, she danced her way to the closed doors. There she came to an abrupt stop, resumed the dignity she deemed proper for a woman of her mature years, opened the door and went on her way, undoubtedly looking forward to a pleasant evening.

I'm willing to venture that she entered the lounge with a smile on her face, and the chances are good that she had an enjoyable evening. I doubt that she spent the evening sitting alone, too shy to speak to anyone and thereby cutting herself off from enjoyment, with or without a dancing partner.

Do we choose, like that woman, to take a chance on what might lie ahead and dance alone to a lively tune? A precious gift from God, life is a dance all the way from birth to that lovely, invisible existence beyond this earth. The joy and adventure of life come to those who hear the sound of God's inspiring rhythms and get up to dance, even though they may do it alone. And whether they can dance in the world beyond their home or in the world within its walls, the tempo they choose will open the door to delightful adventures and new and rewarding experiences.

That has been my own choice, and this book is a sharing of some of the adventures, and a few misadventures, that I have had in my years of dancing alone. Some came as needed lessons, but more came as pure and lasting joy. Many may remind you of your own similar or even very different experiences, and you will enjoy them again as you relive them in memory. All of them have enriched my life, and I hope that they will spur you on to enriching adventures of your own — whether around the corner, far away, or in the one place where all things are possible — your imagination.

Let's open our minds to hear the music of life. And let's keep on dancing . . . until the heavenly chorus pipes us home!

GROWING PAINS

Wishing for the Moon

Once upon a time a girl of twelve was learning
the art of becoming a wallflower. In the gym
of her Chicago suburban school, a party is marking
the completion of the series of dancing lessons
for seventh and eighth graders. The girls sit on
folding chairs along one wall, the boys along the
opposite wall.

"Gentlemen, invite a lady to dance!" the instructor calls out. The "gentlemen" look at one
another and snicker as the instructor walks over
to the Victrola, places a record on the turntable,
and winds the crank on the machine's side. A
few of the bolder boys begin to walk toward the
girls. In a moment the needle scratching is
drowned out by a tinny rendition of "The Sidewalks of New York."

The girl has learned, she hopes, the difference
between a waltz and a fox-trot. She decides this
is a waltz, and she counts mentally, *ONE-two-
three . . . ONE-two-three . . . ONE-two-three.
. . .* She longs to be asked to dance — but what

15

if she steps on her partner's toes?

A boy approaches. She looks down at her sweating hands. He walks past her to the girl in the next chair.

"May I have this dance?" he mumbles, and then the chair to the right of our girl is vacant. She knew he wouldn't ask her! But her heart beats faster and her palms become even more damp, for the boy our young friend has a crush on is approaching. She ducks her head so that he won't see the hopeful look on her face, and surreptitiously she wipes the palm of her right hand on her skirt. He stops. She looks up, hopefully, but he is holding his hand out to the girl in the chair to her left.

There are more girls than boys, and the last reluctant boy has been forced to take a partner. Our girl, squirming a bit on the slatted-wood seat of the folding chair, is one of three girls not asked to dance.

The girl knows she has a good mind, for she was double-promoted in elementary school and is now the youngest in her class and a straight "A" student. Pride in that accomplishment doesn't help her today, however, for "everyone knows that boys don't like smart girls." Besides, she knows she isn't pretty. Her mother still insists that her hair be a Buster Brown bob, while most other girls wear hair ribbons and even corkscrew curls.

"You're as graceful as an elephant!" The girl's violin teacher had said that to her at her last

16

lesson, and that is the part of the half-hour lesson she hasn't forgotten. She is convinced that it is true. If a boy did ask her to dance, she'd probably stumble or not keep step with him! She has learned well the art of becoming a wallflower.

We move ahead a few years. The girl makes the honor roll every month in the large high school she attends, but she is not invited to many social events, nor does she have a boyfriend. Not until she is fifteen and in her junior year.

In the winter months, she and her friend Frances often go ice-skating, a pastime she loves. One day, a boy neither of them knows approaches Frances and takes her mittened hands to skate partners. Deserted, the boy's buddy and the girl are left staring at each other. After an awkward moment, the boy says his name is Stewart.

"We might as well skate," he adds, and reaches out to take the girl's hand. They skate together. She is soon smiling and happy, for she knows she skates well. It is her one area of athletic competence.

"You're a good skater," Stewart says after they glide together the length of the skating area of the lagoon.

"So are you," she says, joy welling within.

When they are making the turn, a sudden misstep sends them both into a fall. They slide along on their bottoms, polishing a path on the ice. But as he helps her to her feet, they both are laughing.

After that day, she watches for Stewart whenever she goes to the park lagoon. He goes to a different school because he lives on the other side of the Garfield Park el, and so she sees him only at the park. But she thinks of him often, and she and Frances go skating almost every afternoon when the weather is right. Stewart often takes the girl's hand to skate even before his buddy starts off with Frances. She has never felt happier.

One of the Chicago newspapers has a page devoted to young people, and a contest invites boys and girls to submit a paragraph describing an ideal friend of the opposite sex. The girl likes to write, so she enters the contest. In her paragraph she describes Stewart without using his name. She titles it "Wishing for the Moon" because she doesn't believe she stands a chance for anything but ice-skating with him. Her little story is published, and she earns her first dollar through writing.

Near the end of that winter, rains spoil the ice for skating, and the girl is disappointed because she misses seeing Stewart. But one day a miracle happens. Stewart telephones and invites her to be his date for a Saturday-afternoon movie in one of the big theaters in the Chicago Loop!

Stewart says, "Can you go? We'll take the el downtown. After the show, maybe we can stop somewhere for a sundae."

Her mother says she may go, and the girl is thrilled and excited — but at the same time nervous. What will they talk about? This is her first date — a great event in any girl's life. She is ready and waiting when he rings the doorbell.

"Stewart's here, Mother! I'm going now!" she calls out, anxious to leave before her parents come into the room. She doesn't wait to hear an answer.

"Hello, Stewart."

"Hi."

"Too bad the ice is melting."

"Yeah. Kind of mushy over there."

They walk the two blocks to the el station with hardly another word, and she is suddenly shy again without the familiar background of the frozen lagoon and ice skaters all around. On the half-hour ride to the Loop, there are periods of silence that seem to go on forever. She becomes more nervous as she tries to think of the right things to say. Stewart seems uneasy too, and both are glad when the time comes to get off the train and descend the steps to Wabash Avenue. A one-block walk to State Street, and the theater is in sight.

He pays the admission, and an usher leads them to two vacant seats on the right side of the center aisle. She takes the second seat, and Stewart the one on the aisle. The short stage show ends and the movie begins. Until then, they have been careful to sit without bodily contact, but Stewart now extends his right arm around the girl's shoulders.

She thinks, *Should I let him do this? Nice girls don't neck!* But she says and does nothing about it, too shy to speak, and liking the touch of his arm on her shoulders.

And then — horrors! The usher comes and taps Stewart on the shoulder. "We don't allow that here," he says, and then departs.

Stewart is terribly embarrassed, and after a minute or two, she says to him, in a trembly voice, "I should have told you — "

He says nothing in reply. There is little said on the long trip home, and no stop for a sundae. He is angry, and he doesn't call again.

She never forgets that first-date fiasco. It is not until years later that she is able to identify the terrible misunderstanding that ruined her budding romance. Stewart had pictured her, not as the shy, inexperienced girl who had never been on a date before, but as one who had "been around." He thought her remark, "I should have told you — " was based on her experience with another boy and that she knew the usher would object to such behavior.

The girl graduates from her big suburban high school and goes to a small teachers' college in Wisconsin. For the first time she is a big fish in a small pond. She hadn't had a chance to work on her high-school paper, even though it was what she most wanted to do. But here, at this small college, in her second year she becomes news editor of the weekly newspaper. She is also elected president of her class and makes top grades in her studies. She graduates at the top of her class and is one of the lucky ones to get a good teaching job in those years of the Great Depression. Her confidence in her mental abilities in-

20

creases — but she has no date for the big class dance.

Adolescence with its mental agonies is almost over, but she still thinks of herself as being "as graceful as an elephant" and is still sure her nose is too big for her to be attractive to young men. On the rare occasion of a date, it is likely to be with a fellow who wants to talk about one of her friends who has jilted him.

I was that girl. The growing pains left long-lasting scars, and it took many years and a variety of demanding experiences for me to grow in social confidence and to see myself as a person worthy of love.

A month or two before graduation from my two-year college course in June 1930, I considered what I should do to support myself for the summer, the interval before the start of my teaching position in early September. In that Depression year, the prospect of a summer job in the Chicago area was extremely slim, even though I had worked there the previous summer in a credit-reference office. So when I learned that an office job was open for the summer at River Pines, a tuberculosis sanatorium about ten miles from the college, with room and board as part of the wages, I mailed off an application.

The opening I applied for was as a typist in the administration office, but when the response came, I discovered that I would also have to take shorthand, which I had never learned. But I was offered work as "second dining-room girl," for room and board and a small paycheck, ten dollars a week. Better than a wasted summer, I decided, and agreed to take the job. I chose to do so rather than be a burden on my parents. I wrote to them of my decision and whereabouts only after I had accepted the offer — and I avoided going into much detail until after I had moved out to the sanatorium, lodging in the big main building above the kitchen and ambulatory patients' dining hall.

I gave no thought to the fact that at River Pines there was a strong possibility that I would be exposed to tuberculosis, still rampant in those years, especially among young adults like me. It just didn't occur to me that I was endangering my own health. Looking back now, I can thoroughly understand the horror my parents felt when my rather tardy and sketchy letter reached them.

The job of second dining-room girl simply sounded as if I'd serve as a waitress. Actually, there were chores assigned that kept me busy from breakfasttime through evening dinner, with an hour off for rest in midafternoon. Often the chores included handling items the patients had used.

Besides serving the ambulatory patients in the dining room, it was my duty to carry meal trays to three of the bedridden patients in a cottage about one hundred feet from the main building. I was instructed to return to the cottage after

22

dining-room work to get the trays and bring them to the kitchen. Often I had to tuck used paper napkins into cups to keep them from being carried away by the breeze, something we were cautioned to prevent. One patient was a girl of about my own age, living in isolation because she was so ill. I'd been handling her trays for two weeks when she died. It wasn't until later, when I was required as a teacher to have a chest X ray and TB scars appeared on the films, that I realized how fortunate I had been not to succumb to TB after so much exposure to the germs.

On one occasion that summer, I was sent to the basement to do some chore in the laundry room. The concrete floor was newly mopped and still wet as I walked toward the light fixture, an old-time, dangling bare bulb with one of those flat, black switches to turn it on. A wicker laundry basket full of bed linens had been left near it. A step beyond the basket I reached up to turn on the light.

Instantly, as the light came on, a pain I've never forgotten went down my right arm and, it seems to me, through my whole body. I distinctly remember feeling the connection from my fingers to my right foot. My fingers seemed fastened to the switch. I know I screamed, and I vividly remember trying to wrench my fingers loose. I stepped backward and fell, breaking the contact. Mercifully, I landed on the pile of sheets in the clothesbasket with my feet extended. No one had heard my scream. I lay there until I recovered enough to get to my feet, shaking with fright.

One seldom sees that type of dangling, unshaded light bulb today, but fear of touching a switch like that one has never left me. Did I write to my parents of this rescue from instant death? No. I discovered years later that they were horrified when they learned of the job I had taken. I can commiserate with them now that I have raised two daughters myself.

I had a third brush with death during my stay at the sanatorium. A friend and classmate who also had a summer job in the area came out to the sanatorium right after we finished our evening work. He had a car and could get around much more easily than I could.

"Hey, Edie, hop in and ride with me," he called. "I've got to drive down to my aunt's house at Friendship, but we can get back before they lock the doors here." Of course I was glad to go, for this young man was my first real love (one that added to my self-esteem problems when it ended with a "Dear Edie" letter some six months later).

While it was still daylight that summer evening, we were on a tree-lined secondary road, off the state highway, when we came to an unguarded railroad crossing. Because of the trees blocking vision to the left, we did not see an approaching train until a sudden blast of its steam whistle alerted us. And there it was, almost on the crossing. My friend was quick-witted and made a sharp right turn off the road, parallel to the tracks.

As the train went roaring past, we sat there on the railroad right-of-way, with the car stopped not ten feet from the passing freight cars, our hearts pounding, adrenaline taking over completely. It was a while before we backed cautiously onto that country road and went on our way.

At that time in my life, my concept of God was still the vengeful "man upstairs" who looked like the bearded patriarch of Michelangelo in the Sistine Chapel in Rome. To me, He was a punishing overlord — distant, unapproachable — rather than the loving Father I turn to today. And I, through many years of my life, carried much guilt — unwarranted, for the most part, but very real to me then.

And yet I know that even in my unenlightened state, God or one of His guardian angels was protecting me. For both before and after that summer my life was not cut short despite foolhardy acts and unexpected dangers. It took a long time for me to realize that, as the Bible teaches, God dwells within each of us, an ever-present help.

Three instances in that one summer of God's loving presence! How can I help but be a grateful believer?

BREAKING OUT OF THE SHELL

From Shyness to Self-Confidence

It is the day after Labor Day, September 2, 1930. I am the new fifth-grade teacher at Hawthorne Elementary School in Elmhurst, Illinois. My nineteenth birthday will be on Friday of this week, and as I look at the children coming into the room one or two at a time, and some with their mothers, I feel totally inadequate. A few of them are as tall as I am!

An upper-grade student comes into the room. He looks around a moment and then walks over to me.

"Where's the teacher?" he asks.

"I am the teacher," I reply, with as much dignity as I can muster, and standing as tall as my five-feet-two frame permits.

After a surprised glance at me, he says, "Oh. Here, Mrs. Waddell sent this." He hands me a typed page.

Since it is from the school principal, I hope it will be a helpful directive for me, but it isn't. All it tells me is what to do with the money I receive for textbooks. My first responsibility is to sell the textbooks, now stacked on my desk, to the pupils (we called the children "pupils" then, instead of "students" as they are now called from kindergarten on). The need to purchase books explains the presence of some mothers of these big fifth graders. I hope those students whose mothers are waiting will get in line first, so that I'll soon be alone with the boys and girls.

When book selling is completed, I am glad to see that all the mothers have been gracious enough to depart, probably wondering what kind of school year their darlings will have under the tutelage of that girl who looks scarcely older than the kids.

With a quick glance, I see that each pupil is seated at a desk — and they're all staring at me. *What am I supposed to say?* I fumble with the book-sale report sheet, but I can stall no longer. The room is quiet, very quiet. The dreaded moment of my having to start being "teacher" has arrived. I get up and walk a few steps.

I stand before the children. *What do I say? What do I have them do now?* I break the silence by introducing myself, and I pick up a piece of chalk and write my name very carefully (penmanship was my poorest subject when I was a fifth grader) on the blackboard. *M-i-s-s S-a-n-s-o-m.* Some look at their friends sitting near them and whisper. I hear giggles, only half suppressed. Then an expectant silence. Ah, yes — I should call the roll. I pick up the list of thirty-two names from my desk.

"Please raise your hand as I call your name," I announce. I try to look pleasant in spite of my lack of confidence as I check off each name.

That done, I am inspired to pick up the list of needed supplies I had found on my desk. I copy it on the blackboard (it was actually a *black*board then, not green).

"Copy the list, please, and bring all these things by the end of the week."

Someone now needs paper. Another child has no pencil. Fortunately, earlier I noticed a small supply of these items in my desk, and I fill the needs. After a few more minutes I am really at a loss. I look up at the big clock on the rear wall above the cloakroom. It is only ten-thirty.

"Please stand," I say, and they all comply.

"You may go home now and come back after lunch," I tell them. They look at one another in surprise and leave the room.

I soon discover my error, for the fourth-grade children are lined up in the hall, taking turns at the drinking fountain and then going back into their classroom. But it is too late to call my class back.

By the time Miss Scott, the well-established fourth-grade teacher in the next room, dismisses her class for lunch, I have had a visit with Mrs. Waddell, who came into my room as soon as word of my error reached her. I received information on school regulations and the answers to some of my questions. Before Mrs. Waddell leaves my classroom, she looks at me speculatively, no doubt wondering how this too-young person is going to handle all those lively fifth graders.

It wasn't easy! I had a lot to learn that hadn't been covered in practice teaching at my college's laboratory school. I stood in awe of the other teachers for quite some time, and especially of Mrs. Waddell, a middle-aged somewhat stout woman. I was far too bashful to go to her and ask for more help.

My shyness with my coworkers at the school was so great that I became almost tongue-tied with all of them, especially the principal. An example:

One day while the children were in the playground, I went into the teacher's room to use the lavatory but saw that it was occupied at the moment. When the lavatory door opened, Mrs. Waddell came out.

"Oh, Miss Sansom — sorry to keep you waiting," she said pleasantly.

As she turned to leave, I saw that her skirt was caught in her girdle, lifted high in back. I tried to tell her, but no words came out and she walked into the school hall that way. I realized how embarrassed she would be, but I couldn't make myself go after her and tell her before the children came along.

How annoyed she must have been at me for not telling her!

While teaching at Elmhurst I was living at my

family's home in Oak Park, paying room and board to my mother from my $100-per-month salary. I had earned enough that summer as second dining-room girl in the tuberculosis sanatorium to buy a 1929 Chevy coupé, $90 total price. The car would enable me to drive to work in Elmhurst in about a half hour.

My salary was $1,200 for the entire school year of 1930–31. Believe it or not, this was the highest-paid elementary-school teaching job offered to anyone in my two-year graduating class at Central State Teachers College! I was most thankful to have been hired at all that year, when many in my class — and in the nation, for that matter — were unemployed.

That annual salary of $1,200 was lowered to $1,100 the next year, because tax-collections were tightening in those worst days of the Great Depression. And before the school year was completed, the municipal coffers were empty. We were given "tax anticipation warrants" in place of the monthly salary check. To convert these warrants to cash, we sold them to a bank at a discount, twenty percent as I recall, in order to have money to meet our living expenses.

When spring came that first year, I didn't realize that we would soon be *really* short of cash, and I couldn't resist buying a brand-new 1931 Chevrolet sport coupé, black with red pinstripe trim, priced at about $900. I loved nice cars then and I still do today! That lovely new car was the joy of my life, with its big saucer-sized hubcaps on wire-spoke wheels, its rumble seat, and its *two* side-mounted "spares," each with a chrome-plated protective cover. In front, the new chrome radiator shield was crowned by a spread-winged eagle radiator cap! How I loved driving that car! I washed it carefully every Saturday.

But sometimes the sportiness of my car made my foot a bit heavy on the accelerator. One lovely spring afternoon soon after I purchased it, I was driving home from school through an adjacent suburb when I noticed a motorcycle cop following me. Then another one pulled just ahead and continued onward not ten feet from my front bumper. Of course, my foot let up on the accelerator. I drove about a half mile with this escort, fore and aft, before I was signaled to stop. The leading officer came to my window.

"Does your mother know you drive so fast, little girl?" he asked.

Pure mortification! I gulped. "No, sir — I mean, yes, sir — "

In the 1930s, in certain states, we didn't have drivers' licenses to show, but he asked me a few questions, wrote down my name and address, and kept me in suspense about having to pay a fine. Still holding his pad and pencil, he looked at me intently. Finally he said, "Little girl, I won't give you a ticket this time, but I'll keep my eye on you."

You can be very sure that I watched my speed after that!

That '31 Chevy was a social asset in the five years that I spent teaching in Elmhurst. My closest friend, Grace, who was a telephone operator, and I wanted to meet young men. Like most young women of that time, we considered marriage, not our jobs, to be our real goal. In the fall of 1932, we were invited to a young-singles church group. Grace and I went solely for social purposes and primarily to meet fellows. We drove to the meeting in my sporty coupé, which was still free of dents and shiny clean.

After the meeting at the church, the group had a custom of going to the home of two of the young men, brothers still living at home with a mother who didn't mind providing some cookies for us. We spent a couple of hours gabbing, dancing, or playing games. Since we were still in hard times, this was the popular mode of entertainment for young adults.

There was a fellow in the group I liked especially, one of the hosting brothers. I hoped he might be interested in me too, but it was the same old story — he was already taken. His girl showed up the second time Grace and I went to the meeting.

Grace and I were sitting side by side on the sofa that night when a fellow they called Mac was standing near. He was nice-enough-looking, but he seemed to be trying too hard to be the life of the party.

"He has a horselaugh, just like Augie," I said

to Grace, referring to a mutual acquaintance we had met elsewhere.

Grace agreed. Mac was staring at me, obviously because of my unkind remark. I thought he was going to say something defensive, but he was looking at me with a puzzled expression.

I was startled to hear him say, "How does a guy get acquainted with a girl like you?" There was no anger in his voice.

A bit confused at this reaction, I said, "Uh, just take the initiative and go ahead!"

Well, to make a long story short, he did. By the time the group was breaking up for the evening, he had arranged for his buddy to drive his old rattletrap car and take Grace along. Mac and I would go in my car, and we'd all meet at a former roadhouse (this was before the repeal of Prohibition) a mile or so away. He behaved well during the rest of the evening, and to my surprise I found he could talk intelligently on number of subjects.

So that is how it began — with a flippant remark on my part. A girl never knows what will turn a guy on!

But Mac, along with eighty percent of the other young men in that group, was jobless. His former employer had been forced into bankruptcy, the economy had not yet begun its recovery the Depression. There simply were no jobs be had for most of the fellows.

When he proposed a few months later, said, "I'll save you from being an old-maid school

33

teacher." I believed him!

We were engaged for two and a half years, awaiting the availability of work for Mac. Couples waited until the man was able to pay the bills — no living together in those days!

He finally found work, earning $21 a week take-home pay. And so Miss Sansom the teacher became Mrs. McCall the day after school closed, June 8, 1935.

There would be a temporary halt in my teaching career when I married, for the school-district had ruled that women teachers were automatically discharged when they married (Mrs. Waddell was the only *Mrs.* on our staff). Men teachers could marry and, in fact, were encouraged to do so. It was blatant sex discrimination — but no one dared fight it. The idea that we should or could oppose it didn't even occur to us. Those were different times in many ways; certainly there was less controversy over individual rights!

I would have continued teaching if allowed to, for employment was just beginning to open up after the worst years of the Depression and we would have to live on my new husband's meager salary. Among my young-woman friends only unmarried teachers and telephone operators were assured of work. Except for a few retail clerks, most of the young men, including Mac, had been jobless until 1934.

We rented a nice apartment for $32.50 a month, and could live on my new husband's salary by being *very* careful. Ten dollars a week was the

household food-and-sundries allotment — but I bought end-of-the-day vegetables and fruit from the store across the street, and the butcher sold good pork chops for ten cents each.

With no job to go to, I was a bit restless, and I soon decided it was time to start a baby despite our meager income. I had an occasional day of substitute teaching in Oak Park — until the day I showed up in a maternity dress. An obviously pregnant woman in the classroom — how scandalous! A small pay raise for Mac was encouraging, and when he got a better job we had the munificent sum of $35 a week.

Mac had an emergency appendectomy that first year, and we worked out a plan with the doctor to prepare his statements (I typed them at my parents' home on their big old office typewriter) for credit against our own bills. In that way we also paid the doctor ($60) for our daughter Connie's very difficult delivery in mid-April 1936.

We continued to exchange work for credit on the doctor's books for several years, until the doctor was doing well enough to hire a secretary-receptionist. We may even have paid in that manner for Mary's delivery on December 31, 1938, our little New Year's gift.

In late 1942, when Connie was six and Mary turning four, we bought a house for about one-third the cost of my present automobile. It was in Western Springs, a pleasant suburb with a good school system. The house was being sold to the highest bidder by the HOLC (the Home Owners'

Loan Corporation) — one of President Franklin D. Roosevelt's "alphabet soup" agencies — which had helped many families to keep their homes during the Depression years. There was little competition for the old place, run-down and with a huge coal-burning furnace, and our modest bid was successful. I learned to hang wallpaper and to paint walls and woodwork, and, as soon as we had the materials, Mac did some carpentry for the girls' room and the living room to provide needed shelving.

In the thirteen years we lived in that house, many things of importance took place. World War II, with its rationing of gasoline and food items, was changing the economy. By 1943, when Mary was about to start kindergarten, I had applied for and been granted an emergency teaching certificate, for now there was a teacher shortage. I was hired for one of the two fourth-grade teaching positions in the elementary school that Connie was already attending and where I'd be nearby as Mary began her school years.

A requirement for certificate renewal when the war ended was that I acquire college credit toward a degree as rapidly as possible. In the summer of 1946 I was admitted to the University of Chicago, Division of the Social Sciences. That was in the time of Chancellor Robert Maynard Hutchins's innovative programs, and I was able to eliminate several courses through passing comprehensive examinations, a real time-saver for me.

Three years later, after intensive work — classes

at night and during summers, and home-study extension courses (the one in physics was the worst!) — I completed the requirements for a master-of-arts degree, bypassing the formality of a bachelor's degree. My M.A. was granted on September 2, 1949, at the famous Rockefeller Memorial Chapel, and presented by Dr. Hutchins at the beginning of his last year at Chicago. To this day I continue to be grateful for his programs, which made it possible for me to attain a master's degree so rapidly after only two years and a summer session of previous college courses.

All those years, my lifetime dream of becoming a writer had been pushed into the background. It emerged forcefully while I was attending a 1946 summer workshop at U. of C., in which most of the students were teachers from a large school district in La Grange, adjacent to Western Springs. Even their superintendent attended when he could. Toward the end of the summer, this group wanted to plan a grand-finale skit, and something inside urged me to volunteer to write it. That I spoke up is an indication of my progress in self-confidence!

The skit was a hit to the extent that the La Grange group asked my permission to perform it again for their board of education, which had sponsored their summer term at the university. My authorship made me known to the superintendent, and the next spring I applied to him for a position in the counseling department. When I promised I'd work toward that degree, I was hired as the district's first reading consultant.

It was writing that helped me get that position, which in turn opened the way for me to become a published author. My first book, the first in a series for handicapped readers, appeared in 1953. It was written as a result of a letter sent to me as reading consultant. The sender asked if I knew someone who might be interested in writing the text for primary-grade science textbooks, in cooperation with science professors.

I waited a week. "I don't know anybody to recommend," I told Mac. "But I'd like to do it myself."

"Well, write that letter," was his reply.

I lost that opportunity because of my hesitation — a person in a position like mine in another school system had been assigned the writing work on the science books.

The letter with that news did not close the door on my opportunity to write, however. It included an invitation to come to the publisher's office and discuss the possibility of writing a new type of book for the beginning reader, a miniature novel in controlled vocabulary. On November 11, 1952, a school holiday, I met with the publishing company president and editor-in-chief. The outcome was my first published book, a pre-primer, in November of 1953. It was the first of a series of twelve small books. They were in print for about twenty years and used in many schools. I had on-going assignments with that company until a corporate take-over in the mid-1980s, when new management changed company policies.

In 1955, with four small books of that first series in print and plans for eight more, I resigned my well-paid position to go out on a limb as a full-time writer and move to the Missouri Ozarks. Of course there were other personal reasons for making the move — primarily my husband's becoming unemployed at age forty-eight and his difficulty finding a new job. My parents had purchased the land on which I now live, and construction of the house I still call home began late in 1955.

Through this difficult time, Mac and I had been growing apart, and we were divorced early in 1963, a year after both daughters, by then college graduates and self-supporting, were married. I have been entirely on my own and living alone for all but less than five years ever since.

As the years passed, a confident person slowly emerged from the shy young woman. Admittedly, there are still times when a bit of my old fear of rejection surfaces and I hesitate to join a group uninvited. But success at my second profession opened a new world to me, and gradually my tendency to withdraw into myself gave way to a new self-confidence.

In recent years, I have made the comforting discovery that self-esteem does not go hand-in-hand with snobbishness or an inflated ego. Rather, a sense of self-worth is an essential ingredient to living a full life.

Even though I have lived alone most of the time since 1963, my life is indeed full. Expanding experiences opened the way for the growth I needed to make the most of latent talent, the talent God built into me and expected me to use.

As we find the circumstances of our lives changing, as occurred in my life, perhaps each of us might find a persistent desire that should be fulfilled, a desire to try something that has a lasting appeal for us. *Persistent* is the key word here, distinguishing the momentary impulse from the true inclination. Perhaps this persistent desire is God's inner urging toward the purposes we were meant for in this life!

One step at a time — that's the way we develop into what God intended we should be. And when we reach that goal and know that we are serving a good purpose, we can feel the inner peace that sustains us, whether we live with a partner, a family, or alone. Our dance of life is then a glissando and often a paean of joy!

WHO'S AFRAID OF THE GREAT UNKNOWN?

Adventures Come in All Sizes

I could hardly breathe, I was so excited! My heart beat in allegro, with a few grace notes thrown in for good measure, as I looked up at the gleaming white sides of the *SS Atlantic.* She awaited her passengers, and I would be among them — Edith McCall from the Midwest, who had never before even been close to an oceangoing ship.

"About to board, miss? Let me take your picture!"

A photographer, who went with us for our whole voyage, was on the job, stopping each passenger about to climb the gangway to board the ship. I still have the picture he took of me that day. It is dated September 5, 1967, my fifty-sixth birthday. (At the time, I considered myself almost beyond middle age — now fifty-six seems quite youthful!) There I am, hair still a nice brown, and with an eager expression on my face as I stand clutching my carry-on bag, raincoat, purse, and identification papers.

That was a long time ago, and I was venturing

out alone on a major vacation trip for the first time. When the *SS Atlantic* moved out of her berth in the Hudson River, she would be bound for the open ocean, en route to that strange-shaped blue area on the European map — the Mediterranean Sea.

For me, 1967 was a milestone year. During five years of living alone, I had worked diligently as a self-employed writer, looking forward to the easing of financial pressures. At last my debts were paid, I had a banner year in royalty income, and I felt it was time to celebrate, to speed up the tempo of my dance of life, to begin my first capital-A Adventure!

The *Atlantic* was not one of those huge ships with thousands of passengers. Her limit was 820, but about 640 were on board for this voyage, and by sailing time, I had already met friendly people. As soon as I went out on the deck, I became acquainted with other first-time travelers. I learned that if I smiled and spoke to people, they seemed just as eager to make friends with fellow passengers as I was.

Late that evening we were all out on deck as the ship made her way down the Hudson, alight with reflections of New York at night. Out in the harbor and off to starboard was the famous Statue of Liberty, her torch lighted, my first view of the Great Lady. And then, minutes later, what a thrill it was to pass under the spectacular Verrazano-Narrows Bridge, new at that time, and the longest suspension bridge in the world! It carried twelve lanes of traffic on two decks for passage between Staten Island and Brooklyn. Seeing that marvelous bridge from the unusual vantage point of going under it made me tingle with excitement.

When table assignments were made, a group of ten of us who were traveling alone were seated at one large table. Instant friendship! David, a bachelor, was the lone male, but he became a friend to each of us. Any remaining concerns about traveling on a ship alone were put to rest later that evening. The Meyer Davis band was playing for dancing in the New World Room. I sat a bit nervously, wondering if I would continue to be a wallflower in spite of those dancing lessons I had taken recently.

Then, wonder of wonders, the ship's white-uniformed radio officer walked over to me. "Would you like to dance?" he asked.

"Yes, thank you," I said, and was on my feet, worried about how well I would be able to follow this man's steps. I had watched his expertise on the floor through one number.

His lead was strong, and I didn't stumble! When the music stopped, he waited for it to start again — and I had a new friend. Hours later, I went to bed in my little inside single cabin, as happy as the proverbial lark.

Eight days on the Atlantic Ocean, enjoyable and luxurious, brought us to Morocco on Africa's northwestern coast. How eagerly I watched as the *Atlantic* moved into the slip reserved for her at Casablanca, whose very name spoke of mystery and romance!

Not wishing to miss a thing, I had purchased the complete package of optional tours offered for this marvelous adventure. We walked to a waiting bus that would take us on a tour of Casablanca and then onward to the Moroccan capital, Rabat. After seeing some of the ancient parts of Casablanca where donkey carts were still common, we headed for the open country. Strangely, most memorable to me were the fences made of sun-baked mud topped with prickly cactus! By way of contrast were the very modern beach cabanas, visible as we went northward parallel to the ocean shore.

In Rabat, I saw the king's palace, which was more like a spacious Hollywood home than my mental picture of a palace. Farewell, fairy-tale concepts! I had a lot to learn — and unlearn!

Highlights of that first great adventure still linger in my memory after twenty-five years and several other voyages. The walled city of old Rabat, the medina, with its Moorish architecture, magnificent mosaics on the walls and gates, and plantings of bright flowers. But an even stronger recollection is of the dark-haired young man at the entrance to the restaurant where we made our lunch stop. He stood there, smiling and greeting us. To this day, I can hear his heavily accented voice as he struggled with the English tongue, and see him, obviously embarrassed, as he pointed down a flight of stairs.

"Lay-dies," he called, smiling sheepishly. He pantomimed hand-washing, and then added, "Et-cet-era, et-cet-era!" We all got the idea!

Impressions: Majorca in the Balearic islands, first port after we went through the Strait of Gibraltar, where we saw the so-called "cell" (studio apartment would be more descriptive) in the monastery where Frédéric Chopin and George Sand lived, with its open balcony and gorgeous view; a tour to the "saw-toothed" mountains east of Barcelona, to the monastery of Montserrat — and our amazement at how laborers could get needed materials for the great cathedral up there, so far from the city below. On to the French Riviera, with its white sand, sun glare, and crowded beaches. Then off to Monaco, where I discovered that the famed casino bore little if any resemblance to those of Las Vegas.

At Monaco, some of us left the ship to go by night train to Rome, an optional side trip. From the depot platform, we could see the harbor below, where the *Atlantic* was docked. It is amazing how attached a person can get to a ship. I had a homesick feeling already! We'd rejoin the ship at Naples two days later.

What a night! The railroad tracks followed the Mediterranean shoreline closely. An aisle ran the length of the sleeping car, and we spent hours at the open windows, drinking in the beauty of the sea under a full moon — waves lapping gently at the shore, dancing sprites of moonlight, our scenic vista only interrupted by the sudden blackness and roar of passing through tunnels from time to time.

I shared a tiny sleeping room with a roommate. I slept in the cramped space of the upper berth, and I've never forgotten my struggle in the morning to get into my girdle when there wasn't room to sit up (we women all wore girdles in 1967).

The glories of old Rome are still with me, but equally strong are other memories, such as the surprise at how spacious and luxurious was the room I shared with another of the ship's passengers in the Hotel Bernini (we could even unlock the door without getting out of the king-size bed) . . . the way the elevator operator stared at us, embarrassing to the point that we used the stairway to our third-floor room to avoid him . . . the noon-hour traffic jam observed from the hotel-room window, so bad that no vehicle could move until several men got off a bus and literally picked up a Volkswagen and moved it out of the way!

I remember Naples, with its nearby Mount Vesuvius and the ruins of Pompeii, of course. Also vivid in memory is the young Italian man who stopped traffic on a wide avenue to help me get across, and then walked me through crowded streets at a breakneck pace to help me find a leather-goods shop. Back at the dock, he suggested I should skip the afternoon Vesuvius tour in favor of going up a mountain to a glove factory and a hotel with him. A flattering proposal for an older woman, and to be taken with a large dollop of salt, just like his statement in broken English, "I pay! I pay!"

Then on to the island of Sicily before rounding the "boot toe and heel" of Italy and eastward to the Aegean Sea and the Greek islands. In Crete, at the ancient palace of the Mycenaean civilization at Knossos, our ship's handsome captain was requested by the photographer to be seated on the stone "throne" in one of the ancient rooms. Captain MacLean said, "I must have a queen beside me!" and beckoned to me. That picture is among my souvenirs.

Then there was whitewashed Mykonos, where I alone dared follow the grizzled Greek miller up the narrow stairway to the loft in one of the many picturesque windmills for a demonstration of the grinding process. After that, there was the island of Delos, birthplace of the mythical sun-god Apollo. Once a busy seaport, now it was inhabited only by caretakers of the irreplaceable ruins. As I walked along the Avenue of Lions, on to a street where the foundations of homes spoke of long-gone residents, I felt a stronger sense of antiquity than I had experienced in Rome. I recall gazing out to the sea from a hillside, noting the lavender hue of the water near the horizon. Then I wandered among pieces of fallen pillars, fashioned by others who saw that same sea so long ago.

My mind teems with recollections of the days that followed. There were the Acropolis and other sights in Athens. Then we moved on to Corfu

47

in the Ionian Islands. There, I walked alone in ancient narrow streets and was snarled at by an imperious cat on a stone abutment. Next, the ship took us into the beautiful Adriatic for a peaceful interlude in Kotor Bay. That was followed by walking in ancient Dubrovnik not far up the Yugoslavian coast. As I write this in 1993, the news is of a war-torn, disintegrated Yugoslavia, and I hope that peace will soon return to those picturesque hillside villages we floated past in the Adriatic before going on to Venice. Yes, I rode in a gondola and heard the gondoliers singing!

On the westward voyage, we made another stop in Morocco, this time at the seaport of Tangier. Stronger than my memory of the Casbah is recollection of our Moroccan-style evening out. We ate dinner sitting on cushions around a table only about a foot high. Mostly, we dipped chunks of bread into a bowl of the strange but delicious concoction called couscous. It was an evening I'll never forget. I even danced with a Nubian, one of a group of entertainers from east Africa. They were wearing beaded headdresses and white robes over blue shirts. Talk about being winded — I certainly was after a lively whirl in a native dance with that Nubian man!

Our last European stop was a visit to the Rock of Gibraltar, where we met the famous apes. I have a picture of a large one sitting beside me on a low wall. I, very gingerly, am feeding a chunk of apple to the ape, and fearing I might lose a finger with the apple. Our last tourist stop was in "the gray Azores," where the clouds seem constantly to cap the mountains. I wonder if Columbus's view was clouded too.

What wonderful memories I have of adventures and sights not described in the travel literature! On the way home, I had another experience I won't forget. I, the former wallflower, was the winner of the ship's cha-cha contest! How 'bout that?

Do you remember the old song "Who's Afraid of the Big, Bad Wolf?" It was the theme of an early Disney movie, based on the children's story "The Three Little Pigs." I think my friends thought I was going into the lair of the big, bad wolf when I said I was going alone to New York to board a ship for a Mediterranean cruise.

"Aren't you afraid to go alone?" I was asked that many times then and afterward when I planned an adventurous trip. The key word there is *planned*. That means taking into consideration the probable incidents and problems that might arise.

In the children's story, the third little pig built his house of bricks, unlike his brothers who used sticks and straw. The brick house was impervious to the big, bad wolf's huffing and puffing to "blow the house down," as he had done to the brothers' flimsy structures. That wise pig based his actions on sound thinking, and his good judgment saved his home and his life. In planning our adventures, we, too, must use good judgment and take actions based on sound reasoning.

A person needs to balance the risks — *real* ones, not those dredged up by someone looking for the worst-case scenario. Good planning makes for confidence, and a confident manner is half the battle. With my "house of bricks" plans made, fear didn't just take a backseat — it didn't even tag along to cloud the prospect of a wonderful time.

I firmly believe that thoughts have power, and that we draw to ourselves the persistent images in our minds. If those images are of unpleasant possibilities, we might soon be saying, like Job of the Bible, "The thing I feared the most has come to pass." If we don't picture the "big, bad wolves" of disastrous possibilities and instead think about the pleasurable probabilities, we are unlikely to meet with the imagined disasters.

The inborn faculty of judgment is a gift of God we employ regularly for successful living, whether young or old, alone or with a partner. If judgment, also known as common sense, tells us that we will lose our home if we spend our cash on a luxury for the sake of adventure, we'd better let common sense prevail!

Yes, I take some chances. We all do, even if we stay at home where accidents can also take place. It's about as risky to take my car out into traffic as it is to cross an ocean in a good ship! When I really want to try something adventurous and *common sense* tells me it does not involve *real* danger, when my *inner voice,* my spiritual

50

guidance, raises no warnings and it seems right for me — it's full steam ahead.

What is an adventure? My dictionary's first definition is "an undertaking of a hazardous nature." Better than that first definition of adventure as "hazardous" (just staying home and opening a can of beans can be hazardous!), I like my dictionary's second offering: "An unusual experience or course of events marked by excitement and suspense." Using that definition, we can have adventures without even leaving home.

To qualify as an adventure, it could even be a vicarious experience that will stimulate the mind, creating excitement and suspense. And mind stimulation is vital to continued alertness as a person ages. Even armchair travelers can have such vicarious adventures if they become truly absorbed in their reading! And today there are wonderful armchair voyages available through VCR films to make us even more involved — and possibly get us so interested that we begin to plan the actual experience.

For that six-week voyage that opened the way to adventurous living for me, I traveled with my mind receptive to excitement and new experiences, ignoring the imaginary big, bad wolves that were possibilities but not probabilities. For example, if I had decided against climbing up the narrow staircase in that old Mykonos windmill for fear of a misstep, or for fear that the Greek miller might harm me when we reached that little loft (possibilities but not probabilities), I'd have missed a unique memory that's in my mental storehouse today.

Those six weeks still add to my vitality after twenty-five years. As you surely can tell, my introduction to dancing alone was a splendid experience!

And here's a delightful footnote to my story of adventure on the *SS Atlantic:* Very recently I received a brochure describing a voyage on a ship small enough to venture into the inland passages along Alaska's coast, where glaciers abound. I had been thinking about just that kind of voyage for some time. A further attraction was that the ship, the *SS Universe,* had a staff of experts to add to the passengers' knowledge of what was seen and experienced.

I became serious about booking a cabin when I read that this ship was the former *SS Atlantic.* After our 1967 voyage, she went into dry dock, then was repaired and sold. Renovated and with a passenger limit of 520, she is now sailing regularly, even on round-the-world winter study voyages. I compared deck plans. Yes, the cabins even carried the same numbers, and I found my 1967 cabin, No. 174! I immediately had an urge to be back on board the ship that had been so special in my life. My next wonderful experience will begin at Vancouver in the summer of 1993, where I'll board the same ship of my first great adventure!

JUST A TOUCH OF IMAGINATION

We Are What We Think

Now I had contracted a lifelong case of sea fever. I enjoyed the shipboard activities, of course, but what enchanted me most was just being out on the ocean. I delight in looking aft and seeing the creamy wake of a ship on an intensely blue sea, watching the water alongside the ship break into intricacies of crocheted lace foam. What pleasure it is to spend idle hours watching for ships on the horizon, for the graceful ballet of dolphins, for changing hues in stormy sky and water! And when the ship docks, to see the world up close — not just under clouds as it is so often viewed from an airplane. This was — and still is — my dream.

So it was less than two years after my *Atlantic* odyssey that I signed up for another cruise, this time a Caribbean voyage, embarking January 6, 1969. I had writing assignments to complete, so I could not be away as long as I had been on that first trans-Atlantic cruise.

But this adventure fell short of satisfying my

expectations. As Caribbean cruises go, it was fine. The problem lay with me, for I compared it to my lovely Mediterranean experience, which covered many more miles at sea. To start with, we flew from Miami to Haiti, where we boarded the ship, and also flew back from the islands. There was little time for just enjoying the ocean vistas other than the first day, when we cruised from Haiti to the island of Curaçao in the Venezuela coastal area, and one other day as we headed for the Windward Islands. The routine was to embark at night and by dawn we'd be anchored at our next port of call, where we'd stay all day.

Our daily tours were fascinating. Curaçao was almost a desert island when it was captured from the Spanish by the Dutch in 1634, but the pioneer farmers thought that they might be able to grow oranges. However, the orchards produced only small, rather bitter fruit. Ingenuity led the planters to discover they could use their disappointing crop to create the liqueur named for the island. They must have been a rather clever group of founders, for they also made it possible for ocean-going ships to dock right in the heart of the city of Willemstad, capital of the Netherlands Antilles. Canny, those Dutch pioneers!

But most of the islands were the vision of tropical loveliness that cruise passengers dream of, ringed in enticing white sandy beaches — except for one of *black* sand that was a novelty but not inviting. We saw mountainside fields of banana trees, which aren't really trees at all but huge, overgrown stalks with flowers that grow into great clusters of green, upside-down bananas. After but one harvest, the plant dies and must be replaced. There were also plantations of other lush, tropical crops growing in mountainside fields.

The steel-drum bands that greeted us from the dock at most ports as the ship, the *SS Dalmatia* of Yugoslavia, arrived were fun to hear and to see. Even more delightful for me was a personal serenade composed and performed by two calypso singers on the island of Trinidad, against a background of palms and the sea. The island inhabitants were nearly all charming, although the extreme contrast in living conditions for the few wealthy and the countless poor was disturbing.

As on the *Atlantic*, I was welcomed into a group assigned to a large table in the dining room, so I wasn't lonely or left out of tour groups. The table and tour mate I remember most vividly (but definitely not in a romantic way!) is a man I'll call Harold, the bachelor among us. He had a habit of constantly checking his watch, as if time mattered that much. That's what he is doing in the only snapshot I have of the group!

Harold had another flaw from my viewpoint — he had little sense of adventure. At La Guaira, the port city for Caracas in Venezuela, we were offered the opportunity to ascend by funicular to the top of Mount Avila for a spectacular view of the city below and the bay beyond La Guaira. It was my first chance to ride up a mountainside in one of those suspended cars, and I was eager to go — and did, despite Harold's advice to remain on the ground. He told us the cable would probably break and drop us to certain death. Most of us went anyway. It was easy to see why Harold was still a bachelor. Poor man!

I was doing some research for the elementary-school social studies textbooks I was coauthoring at the time, so in Port of Spain on the island of Trinidad, in place of the standard tour, I took a special-request taxi tour. I asked the driver to take me to a public school. He drove me to a sprawling one-story square building with wood siding that reached only halfway up the classroom walls. The upper half was open to the outside air, with no window screens. I have a photograph I took of some children (all well-behaved) and their teacher on the school grounds. The attractive young teacher wears a white blouse and bright yellow skirt. The little girls are in an aqua uniform dress, and the slender boys all wear white shirts over shorts in a variety of colors.

That voyage satisfied my curiosity about the very popular Caribbean cruises, and I've never had a desire to sign up for another one. For my dance of life, I would need to find another mode of ship travel, less staccato and more of a lovely glissando, without the constant feeling of being at a party.

Your idea of adventure may be entirely different from mine. Maybe you would like the floating-party life-style so much that you'd immediately begin to plan your next Caribbean cruise. I know some people who enjoy every moment and repeat the experience whenever they can. That's great for them, for the planning and actual voyages stimulate minds and bodies. It is highly unlikely that they will become couch potatoes!

But perhaps, for you, the very thought of ship travel brings on vertigo. Your idea of adventure may be mountain climbing, or finding a rare antique, or learning a foreign language or how to use a computer. Maybe you're a homebody and would prefer never having to go far from home to feel the excitement of doing something adventurous. It is well that we choose different tempos for our dance of life. What a crowded dance floor we'd have if we all found satisfaction in the same life-style!

Fortunately, however, we are alike in that each of us is created with certain inborn faculties, and one of them is the imagination. Using our imagination can make an adventure of something so simple as going to a shopping mall. Or we can embark on armchair traveling, imagining ourselves on a mountain-climbing expedition as we read about it or see a video. Our imagination can take us on visits to strange, exotic places. We can even imagine ourselves getting behind the wheel as owner of our dream car.

"Wow!" we say. "Wouldn't that be something great to really do? I wonder if I could. . . ."

Maybe we can! It can become a stimulating goal. The power of imagination should always be used in a positive way, never for dreaming up negative scenarios. Used positively, the imagination is a blessing. Used negatively, it can be a handicap. For science is proving that we are what we think. Our thoughts can affect our bodily health as well as our mental health.

Mental and physical stimulation are part of having a good life in our later years. They help to ward off the debilitation we all dread. Even if our desire remains an unrealized dream, using the imagination to envision it is stimulation. It diverts our mind from the signs of physical aging, and actually slows those signs, for mind and body work together. Goal setting, "imaging" what we desire, gives us the motivation to strive toward a fuller and more enriched life, a life that will never be boring.

"Follow your bliss," Joseph Campbell, the philosopher and mythologist, advised us. He himself did, and lived a productive life almost to his dying day at the age of eighty-three. Our thoughts are powerful, and what our minds conceive we may achieve. The idea came first, even to God in the great creation of this earth and everything on it!

To picture ourselves achieving a goal is not idle daydreaming. It is making use of a powerful tool available to us all. More and more, we see reports of people using the power of imagination in a positive way to maintain or even restore good physical health. Just get to know a man or woman still mentally and physically active at ninety! The likelihood is that he or she is a person who dwells on the positive, giving little time or thought to the negatives that pop up in everyone's life. Such people are inspirations to us all, showing us what is possible — even if we dance alone.

MAGIC CARPETS

Our Own Private Genies

Do you remember the story of Aladdin, the poverty-stricken lad with the lamp he found deep in a subterranean chamber? When he rubbed it, a genie appeared and transported him via magic carpet anywhere he chose. On that voyage on the *SS Atlantic*, crossing the ocean for the first time to geography-book lands, I felt almost as if I, too, had acquired a genie of the lamp and a magic carpet to carry me away in my mind to other times and places. I feel I still have magic carpets for return visits — magic-carpet voyages without leaving home.

These magic carpets are the special souvenirs I've brought home over the years, beginning with that first time I danced alone. A wonderful thing about them is that they enable me to relive adventures, no matter how many years have passed since the actual experiences. I need only walk into my living room and pick up a small music box to be transported to an ancient city in Morocco. I have a lovely carved shepherd's cup that takes me to Yugoslavia. I can also go to Rome, to Corfu, or to the Azores — just walking around my house.

I wish you could see that Moroccan music box! It's rectangular, four inches wide by almost six inches long, and stands about two inches high. The top is inlaid in a most intricate pattern, like a miniature of the marvelous mosaics of ancient Moroccan architecture. The colors of the tiny inset design portions range from dark brown to ivory, with accents of soft coral and a few chips of mother-of-pearl.

It takes me back to where I found it, in a tourist shop in the old section of Rabat, Morocco. It was one in a jumble of similar boxes on a table, priced so low I could scarcely believe it. But many of them were missing important parts of the inlay, and I had to hunt a bit to find this particular box. Its inlaid chips were all in place on the top and sides except for one small piece of the border design, and it played a tune when I wound its mechanism and lifted the lid. But two of the wooden-ball feet were missing. I rummaged about for loose feet, found two, pushed in the pegs that held them in place, and paid for my treasure.

That music box can do more than arouse memories. It is an example of how a souvenir can stimulate a person's mind, which is vital to keeping that dance of life continuing past three score and ten. The day I found the box is long gone, but to this day that souvenir charms me, not just for the intricacy of design and excellence of workmanship, and not just because it conjures up my entire Morocco adventure, even to dancing with the Nubian man. After I'd listened to it many times, my curiosity about that little tinkling tune was aroused and I was off on my magic carpet for new mental flights.

The tune that the little brass cylinder and flexible prongs play is one I've never heard on music boxes sold in American stores. Inside the box, in raised letters on the metal casting that holds the controls is "Switzerland," plus a song title — "Jura Song."

Jura? To the big dictionary! The lower-case form of the word is the plural of *jus*, I learn. What does *jus* mean? It's Latin for law. Right below *jura* I see capital-J *Jura*. Now we have it! This refers to the Jura Mountains between France and Switzerland. That makes sense. This is a song of the Jura region, perhaps an area whose boundaries were established by some judge. Maybe I'll track that one down sometime.

Now I'm riding my magic carpet on one of those armchair adventures, with my imagination and curiosity at full speed ahead. Looking up *Jura* in my encyclopedia, I learn that as the Swiss forest lands were cleared, home industries developed in the valley villages, among them watchmaking and obviously also the related manufacture of music-box mechanisms, some of which were shipped to Morocco — my treasure among them.

But on the inside of the lid where there is more inlaid design, there is also a sticker giving a French name for the tune, "La Petite Diligence." This French phrase reminds me that I had once read of Morocco's relations with France, from the time of the Berber invasion in about 730, through the years of Morocco as a French colony. When did that end? To my encyclopedia again. Morocco became independent in 1956, at the beginning of the great period of withdrawal of colonial rule and founding of new nations all over the continent of Africa.

I look again at that French title: "La Petite Diligence." From my high-school French, I know that *la* is a feminine article for the noun that follows. *Petite* is the feminine form for *little*. My French-English pocket dictionary, saved from high-school days, tells me *diligence* has a French meaning the same as the English definition — sticking to the job at hand "with all due speed." But there is another meaning, which I discover was also used in English-speaking lands — a *diligence* was a type of horse-drawn coach.

So now I have a picture in my mind to go with that short, tinkling melody — a ride in a tiny, old-fashioned pony cart through the foothills of the Jura Mountains. As the little brass cylinder turns, I can fairly hear the horse prancing along a bumpy road. With all that I've learned through curiosity aroused by my souvenir, I would not have that little tinkling tune exchanged for a lovelier one, nor would I ever consider including the music box in a yard sale — or even selling it for much more than its trifling cost! It will be among my heirlooms when I depart this world.

From two visits to Yugoslavia and the voyage on that Yugoslavian ship, *Dalmatia*, I have some beautiful and interesting woodcarvings to bring that land to mind. My favorite is the shepherd's cup from the ancient walled city of Dubrovnik. Graceful in line, it is one of seven woodcarvings I bought for less than twenty dollars on that 1967 Mediterranean trip.

That painstakingly carved cup is symbolic of peaceful days in Yugoslavia, a far cry from the reign of terror there as I write. My imagination takes me to the tranquil times when shepherds passed the hours with carving while they tended their sheep on those grassy mountainsides near the Adriatic Sea, idyllic days that may never return.

Because of my Yugoslavian magic carpets, I take a much greater interest in developments there — and it is a real challenge to follow the "who, why, where, and when" of the changes. But a challenge is what we need to keep us from letting our life dance wind down to a dirge!

On my end table there is a triangular, white ceramic ashtray. It's a magic carpet to Rome, with its classic ruins and its modern traffic jams — plus a reminder not to become too smug about my strength of character! The ashtray has on it, in green, a reproduction of the Bernini fountain in the Piazza Navona. I was charmed by Rome's fountains — and with the ashtray when I saw it on a table in the Hotel Bernini. When it was time to check out, I packed it in my suitcase with every intention of paying for it at the checkout desk. Honest! But the desk clerk, austere in formal morning coat and striped trousers, had such an expression of disdain on his face that I lost my courage to tell him I had it — and thus I became guilty of theft. While the ashtray brings back memories of Rome's marvels, it is also a humbling reminder of my good intentions that fled before that desk clerk!

The little golden-wire sailing ship on a mantel shelf recalls to my mind the sight of the gray Azores — gray because clouds seem drawn, as if magnetized, to form a blanket of mist that nests almost constantly over a pair of beautiful volcano-crater lakes. I'm sure the clouds were there when Columbus cried out, "Sail on, sail on and on!" They covered the lakes when the *SS Atlantic* took us there in 1967, and they veiled the islands again when I glimpsed the Azores from a freighter in 1990.

The little ship is modeled after the *Santa Maria*, and I think of the courage of Columbus and of his strong conviction long before the oceans were mapped that he would find China if he sailed westward. How did he feel as he left the security of the Azores and went on into the vast unknown of the seas? More than as a discoverer, he's to be honored for his courage to act on his own convictions, to dare the great unknown on faith.

His discovery of the New World was accidental, but his faith and courage were monumental.

There's one more souvenir among my large assortment that I must mention. In my china cabinet stands a wine-red plate (made in Genoa, Italy, Columbus's hometown) with the *SS Atlantic*'s shipping-company name and emblem on it in gold. It's a great magic carpet to self-esteem, because it reminds me that even an old dog can learn new tricks — I won that plate for dancing the cha-cha!

Most people want to know how to live long and happy lives. But many are the forty-year-olds, or even the "thirty-somethings," who see those first small laugh lines and turn to the cosmetic ads for an antidote. Why? Because they consider facial lines to be wrinkles, and everyone knows that wrinkles mean you are getting old! Worrying over the appearance of a few wrinkles is a good way to breed more of them. Besides, lines gained through cheerful, purposeful living give a person's face character and interest to replace the blandness of youth.

Over and over again we read that an active mind, coupled with physical activity and a strong belief in a caring God, are far more essential to achieving a long and happy life than anything from the cosmetic counters.

Mental activity helps keep boredom away as we advance in years, compensating in some measure for diminishing physical abilities. Think of people you know who are aging gracefully. In all probability, they are among the more interesting of your acquaintances, because they have active minds and many interests.

A panel of healthy people past eighty-five was asked on a TV talk show, "What do you think is keeping you active year after year?"

"I don't think about how old I am — got too much else to do," was one reply.

Another commented, "See the bright side. Some people spend all their time looking for what's wrong with things and the world. I keep looking for the good things — and I find them too."

Often, our well-intentioned sons or daughters, who have not yet learned that to be over forty is not synonymous with the onset of a helpless old age, are concerned that their parents might be straining themselves by trying something new. A friend of mine, a woman in her early sixties, would like to learn to use a computer. Knowing she aspires to be a writer, her son is trying to steer her away from the sometimes-frustrating process of learning to use a multipurpose computer and wants her to settle for a glorified electronic typewriter, now called a word processor.

"Why make it harder for yourself, Mom?" he asks her.

But one of the best things "Mom" could do would be to work her way through the details of operating a computer and being able to install into it whatever programs she fancies in addition to word processing. For example, I have a new computer program that is rebuilding my French vocabulary and ability to read French with understanding. I may never need it, but it feels just great to regain the abilities I had long ago after four years of French in high school. My friend is the type who would appreciate a computer's possibilities — and when she learned to operate it in a few days, the stimulation of success would be a nonmedicinal tonic for good health.

Our caring offspring do not always realize how capable their elders are and that we can still find satisfaction in new accomplishments. By setting realistic goals for ourselves, not only do we gain the satisfaction of accomplishment, but we also are involved in an antiaging process as important as a routine of physical exercise.

"Curiosity killed the cat," the old saying goes, but to a human being, curiosity can be a stimulus to richer living and a longer life span. If we have enough curiosity and desire to learn, chances are we'll never succumb to being couch potatoes, with eyes for nothing more fascinating than a rerun of an old TV sitcom.

So while we can still get up and dance, let's look for opportunities to enrich our lives. And we won't let our well-meaning relatives tell us we can't learn new tricks. We *can* if we want to! Like Aladdin, let's rub our magic lamp of curiosity and ride away on a magic carpet. . . .

FROM CABOCHONS
TO PINK CHICKENS
Opening the Door for Opportunity

At my brother's home one day in the early 1970s, I saw a publication with the intriguing logo *TravLtips*. "Where did you get this?" I asked.

"Oh, I sent for that," Jack replied. "Marie and I were thinking that when I retire we'll go on one of the freighter trips it tells about."

As it turned out, *I* went on one of those freighter trips while Jack and Marie were still thinking about it. I had found what I was seeking. I subscribed to *TravLtips* for myself. Eagerly, I read each issue of the little magazine cover to cover. Most of the published pieces were accounts of voyages on cargo ships written by the passengers themselves.

Invariably, the authors mentioned the pleasure that passengers took in watching the cargo-handling processes. Often, all of them went up to the bridge deck, the open area at the highest level of the ship's "house," as the multistoried structure is called. From up there, they could look down into the cavernous open holds, as well

69

as see the docks from which freight was being loaded.

The writers told of seeing boxes, bales, barrels, rolls of newsprint — a multitude of items stacked on pallets and brought shipside by forklifts. The pallets were skillfully lifted by cranes and lowered into the holds. Cranes also picked up automobiles and lowered them into specially equipped holds where workers secured them against moving about.

The logo for *TravLtips* has the name enclosed between the fore and aft sections of a ship with cranes bristling from the decks. This logo depicted the silhouette of a typical oceangoing cargo ship in the '70s, when bulk cargo was still the rule, and before nearly all cargo was stowed into those huge metal boxes called "containers," as is done today.

Not all freighters accepted passengers. *TravLtips*, of course, dealt only with the cargo ships that had passenger accommodations. Some ships took as few as four passengers, and there were never more than twelve on a voyage. The reason for the passenger limit was that maritime law required a ship with more than twelve persons, not including crew members, to have a physician on board, and to pay him whether or not any passenger needed his services.

I also discovered that becoming a passenger on a cargo ship was like becoming a member of a temporary family. Passengers shared tables in a dining room, often one large table. Their meals and the ship's officers' meals were usually served in the same room. One dining-room steward (often the same person who was passenger-room steward) was assigned to serve the passengers, and the service was generally excellent. The reports varied in enthusiasm for the food quality, but all spoke of more than ample quantity.

Every freighter also seemed to have a room where passengers gathered for relaxation, furnished with a refrigerator so that passengers could have between-meal snacks. There were comfortable chairs for reading, a library of books, and tables for playing games, working jigsaw puzzles, or whatever the passengers chose. In the evening, the passengers were sometimes invited to watch movies on a TV set. (Today all freighters have a VCR and a library of movie tapes.) When they were in port, passengers could always go sightseeing together, and when on shipboard between expeditions, watch the fascinating unloading and loading procedures.

In the magazines, there were photos of passenger cabins. They were invariably much larger than the two I had occupied on cruise ships, and always outside locations. Most had windows rather than portholes, and every cabin had a private bath. The authors praised the passenger-room steward for taking wonderful care of the cabin and of all their needs. This steward was usually male and of foreign birth but English-speaking, friendly, and helpful.

And the stories of visits to faraway ports! I

loved to read them, with all the details of places to go, of the small tour taxis that were always available and would take groups of four who could share the cost — fascinating! At that time, a voyage often included at least two- or three-day stops at ports, which allowed the passengers plenty of time for local sight-seeing.

When the ship was a short distance from a port where docking was scheduled, all the passengers usually were out on deck to watch the approach of a small motor launch. On board the launch was a harbor pilot who would be responsible for guiding the ship the rest of the way to its assigned dock space. As the launch came alongside the big cargo ship, the harbor pilot stood ready to transfer to the huge ship without the launch coming to a full stop. He always entered the big freighter via a door opened on the deck just above the waterline — a precarious transfer! Some of the ship's crew stood by, ready to grasp his hand and make sure he got on board. He was escorted immediately to the bridge, from which the ship was steered.

Away the launch went with a swish and a foamy wake, and very soon a pair of tugboats would be seen approaching the behemoth moving slowly toward the port, now with its propeller at rest. By this time, all the passengers were out on deck and leaning over the rails to see the two tugs, each tied to the ship by heavy ropes ("lines," in proper seafaring lingo). Pushing and pulling, the tugs conducted the freighter to the area assigned to it on a freight dock.

I was entranced. In the spring of 1978, when I felt financially able to pay for a voyage and free to be away for several weeks, I called the *TravLtips* booking office to be waitlisted. I had chosen a shipping line that went from New York to South American countries via the Panama Canal. My excitement rose to fever pitch when a woman from the office called me on September 12 to offer me one of the two single cabins on Voyage 3 for 1978 of the twelve-passenger *Delta Venezuela*.

"This cabin just became available. The ship's scheduled for September twenty-second from Brooklyn. Can you make it?"

"Yes, yes!" was my reply. I certainly *would* make it! I started to pack immediately. I had already prepared for this eventuality with the required good-health certificate and a valid passport. I'd take care of such matters as bill paying, pick-up of my mail, etc., and get on my way, driving as far as my daughter's house in Pittsburgh, where I'd leave my car and fly into La Guardia Airport. I had my pier information and would taxi from the airport to the ship.

Freighter passengers are always advised to inform the travel agent as to where they can be reached for last-minute information, and I had given my daughter's phone number. When I reached her house on September 20, the call had already come confirming that the ship would leave on September 22, and I could board between one and three P.M. With a plane reservation made, I was all set!

The *Delta Venezuela* was scheduled to make nineteen port calls, five of them on the outward-bound segment along the East Coast. Our last United States stop would be at Miami before we headed for Santo Domingo, our first foreign port, and on to Colombia. We'd go as far as Ecuador after transiting the canal, and could expect to get back to Brooklyn "on or about October 23." It turned out to be October 26 even though, loaded with bananas, we made an extra-fast return voyage from Guayaquil, Ecuador, and Buenaventura, Colombia.

I have come to think of freightering as mental and physical therapy. It allows a person to become completely detached from the pressures and stresses of everyday life, with as much opportunity for meditation as she wishes. On a freighter, one is freed from the frantic tempos of life in the '90s.

When I went on that first trip, my only contact with my normal world was when mail came for me at the addresses furnished by the shipping company and, also, two rather exciting occurrences — messages that came via the radio officer. The information we left with family and business contacts had included radiogram instruction. To me, freightering was an ideal way to vacation.

Traveling via freighter is soul medicine, in more ways than in offering the opportunity for detachment from normal life pressures and also time to meditate. In order to be a "happy camper" on a freighter, you have to work at developing *patience* and *flexibility,* two qualities essential to a life of peace and good health under any circumstances, even when at home.

Patience must be exercised because freighter voyages are not scheduled for the passengers but for cargo. Once you have made a voyage choice, patience is required until you learn of available space. Sometimes you are waitlisted for more than a year! Then comes the word of the time frame within which the ship is likely to sail, and the estimated number of days of the voyage. Both are subject to change. Patience is needed all through this waitlist period, and sometimes even after you travel to the port where you are to board the ship, you may have to wait in a motel or hotel until it arrives.

Flexibility! Freighter traveling is not for the person who cannot adjust to changing plans and schedules. It requires that we accept the fact that the cargo handling takes precedence over our sight-seeing plans. We may have been told that our ship will be in port for two days, and we arrange our sight-seeing plans accordingly. But then the captain gets dock service ahead of schedule — so our time in that port is cut to one day. The captain is required to keep expenses as low as possible, and efficient handling of the cargo is his responsibility. The cargo, not the passengers, comes first.

Passengers must also be self-sufficient in what we will do with our time between ports. Yes, there are movies to see, but other than that, passengers entertain themselves — walking the decks, playing games, conversing, reading, writing a diary, needlework brought from home, or my favorite pastime, just watching the sea from a deck chair. Wonderful for dreaming and meditating!

No, freightering is not for everyone. Besides patience, flexibility, and self-reliance, there are physical requirements. A passenger must be in good health and able to climb stairs — lots of them. The first long flight is up the gangway to get aboard — forty-some steps. Then there's the climbing from deck to deck, because it is a rare freighter that has an elevator. But that's an advantage too — you can eat the abundant fare and not gain an ounce!

For some of us, freightering is the capital-A Adventure. The unexpected aspect of what will happen and how the itinerary might change only makes it more enjoyable for the true freighter enthusiast. Once a freighter buff, always a freighter buff!

My cabin on the *Delta Venezuela* was huge — about sixteen feet long and twelve feet wide — with two square windows, not portholes! One corner of the room was devoted to a bathroom, larger than the little ones on most cruise ships.

"Captain Smith says to welcome you aboard, Mrs. McCall. My name is Lloyd," the steward said when he had brought my luggage to my cabin. After it was all in place, he picked up a thermos carafe from the dresser and went out into the corridor. When he returned with it, he said, smiling, "This is your drinking water — don't drink that stuff from the bathroom faucets. We want you to stay healthy and enjoy this trip. If there's anything you need, just let me know."

When Lloyd had left, I hurried to the window. Down the river a short way, I could see a ferry taking on passengers, and beyond, to the south, stood the Statue of Liberty. Hastily, I did some unpacking — I had plenty of drawer space and two lockerlike closets for hanging my clothes. Then I could wait no longer to get out on the deck.

Some of the other passengers were out there too, watching the cargo loading. We smiled but didn't try to talk, for the air vibrated with the clatter of the many small forklifts scurrying about and the screech of cranes reaching in all directions. Crates, bales, and bundles were piled on the square wooden pallets, and we watched as the cranes lifted them with ease and then lowered them into an open hold below the high deck from which we watched.

We were still watching when a gong called us to our first meal on board and a chance to meet one another. We ten passengers were from Texas, Indiana, Michigan, New York, and Missouri. Two of the four married couples on board were old friends; the other single cabin was occupied by the sister of one of the wives. The two other couples and I were strangers to all — but only very briefly. I, the one from Missouri, was the only person who had come alone, but I was immediately part of the group. By the second day we had become a family of ten.

About seven-thirty, loud blasts on the ship's horn announced we were ready to move out. The holds had been covered, cranes folded, and deck cargo anchored in place. The harbor pilot was on board, the lines pulled in, the anchor lifted, and a pair of tugs moved in to start us down the river.

The Great Lady in the harbor was still visible through the mists of a drizzly dusk as the *Delta Venezuela* glided toward the Upper Bay. All ten passengers were out on deck. We passed under the Verrazano-Narrows Bridge, its strings of lights gemlike in the mists. Blackness seemed to hem us in as we went on, the dark depths of the water broken by two guiding rows of lighted buoys — red to port and green to starboard.

And so began a memorable voyage.

We weren't exactly on the open sea for all that first week of our voyage, for the very next day we were taking on cargo at Philadelphia and on Sunday we were docked at Baltimore, which we reached via the inland waterway. By the end of the week we had also visited Newport News and Charleston, and made a final United States stop at Miami. The approach to cities from the waterways was novel, a view not possible from land transportation, and each time we "supervised" the docking until lines were cast and the tugs scurried away like big waterbugs.

We took buses or subways to see the various historic places: in Philadelphia, Independence Hall, where our nation's Founding Fathers had met; in Baltimore, the waterfront park where, outside the park building, a huge eighteen-star flag flew, a replica of the one that Francis Scott Key saw over Fort McHenry when he was inspired to write "The Star-Spangled Banner" during the War of 1812. We passed Fort Sumter, in the harbor at Charleston, where the first shots of the Civil War were fired, and then, on shore, we toured the nearby historic district. We passed the U.S. Navy yards, viewing them as they can be seen only from the sea, and later viewed the row of impressive white hotels along the beaches on the approach to Miami.

At each stop, we took on more cargo: automobiles for Servicemen in Panama; a huge machine for bottling Coca-Cola destined for a South American city; barrels of chemicals; bales and bundles of various items. Each time we moved on, the *Delta Venezuela* rode a little deeper in the water.

Along the way, we passengers had come to know the ship's officers too. They were a sociable group. Our captain, Kenneth G. Smith, was a big man, usually dressed in a jumpsuit instead of a uniform. He, the purser, and the chief steward made frequent shopping trips ashore to stock the ship with needed items and groceries for our five-week voyage.

One day Shirley, my new friend from Detroit, and I were down on the U.S. Army dock near Charleston. We were watching the loading of automobiles into the ship's holds when Captain Smith hailed us and asked, "You two want to go to a shopping center?" He and the chief steward were walking toward a waiting car.

We both were definitely interested. I was already aware that my walking shoes were not going to be adequate for the long voyage ahead, and I wanted to buy another pair. But my purse was in my cabin.

"Do I have time to go up to my cabin to get my purse?" I asked. "I'd like to buy a pair of shoes."

But the captain said, "Don't worry, here's a fifty. Let's go." And he handed over the currency, which was more than adequate in those preinflation years. Away we went! Of course, I paid Captain Smith back that night, but my friends still tease me about the captain who bought me shoes.

This ship was unique in that Captain Smith, a lapidary by avocation, had all his equipment on board. One evening soon after we were out at sea, he invited all the passengers to his suite for cocktails and to show us his wide variety of rough-cut semiprecious stones. The grinding wheels and fine-work equipment were in his suite, and after showing them to us, he demonstrated the art of making cabochons from rough-cut stones, for mounting in rings or pendants. Then he offered to instruct any of us who wished to try our hand at the art with pieces of the less-expensive materials.

Never one to neglect such an opportunity, I was soon working on a piece of stone of mottled gray and lapis lazuli blue. I learned to shape it into an oval that could be set in a silver ring. As a result, I have a ring whose sentimental value is far greater than its monetary worth. The finishing work was done by Captain Smith.

The ever-present writer in me jumped at another opportunity: I interviewed the captain and took photographs of him working at his hobby. As soon as I reached home, I wrote "He Takes His Hobby to Sea." The article was published in the May 1979 issue of *Lapidary Journal*, illustrated with four photographs I took of Captain Smith working in his quarters on the ship and one he snapped of me as I worked on my project.

We left Miami on Friday, September 29. Days at sea were filled as each person chose, but Ruth, one of the passengers, had brought supplies for each of us women to make a small, quilted cushion cover from printed and padded fabric. We sewed and talked, stopping often to observe the ever-fascinating sea, and always alert for porpoises or dolphins, which sometimes appeared off the prow doing their lithe, harmonious water ballet. In the evening, the captain and the purser showed us movies in the lounge.

"All we need now is the popcorn," one of the

passengers remarked. And off went the purser, soon to return with bowls of freshly popped corn!

Our first foreign port was Santo Domingo, where we arrived after sunset and left before dawn, staying just long enough to unload cargo. We passengers preferred not to leave the ship in the dark of night, knowing nothing about the place. As it turned out, watching the scene on the dock from a deck was enough entertainment for us.

I've been out watching the unloading of cargo from the hold of this ship to the Santo Domingo freight dock, I wrote in my journal at ten-fifty P.M. that night. *It was like a disorganized circus going on down there! Santo Dominicans were driving forklifts helter-skelter all over the dock, dodging the square wooden pallets of cargo lowered by the big cranes, and somehow managing to get them onto the lifts and into the warehouse.*

We held our breath when the cranes lifted a twenty-foot-long steel container from the deck and lowered it onto an oversized forklift. We screamed as the container teetered dangerously, extending out in both directions over the heads of the milling workers. The driver, seeing smaller forklifts in his way, raised the platform to its highest point. The container almost fell from its high perch several times, but on he went with it. We held our breath again until the container teetered its way around a corner of the warehouse and disappeared into the night.

All this time, bulk unloading also went on — bundles of long-handled scoop shovels, rolls of fabric and linoleum, boxes and bales of who-knows-what — all stacked onto hand trucks or dollies. Loads were often spilled as the workers, shouting to one another in Spanish, rolled the dollies away from the ship en route to the warehouse, about 150 feet from the ship. Frenetic is the word for the whole scene!

In the midst of all this mad activity, a man came onto the dock pulling a vehicle like those trainmen used years ago to take baggage from the cars. This fellow had large cans of some kind of drinks and a block of plastic-wrapped ice on the cart. He dumped the ice out on the dirty wagon bed, chopped it into small chunks, and dropped ice, debris and all, into the cans of whatever liquid was in them. Then he dispensed his concoction in Styrofoam cups to the workers, who seemed pleased to buy it. It was a crowning touch to the great circus performance viewed from our observation platform on the ship.

The next day, Sunday, October 1, we had a special event at sea — the ceremony of sending into the deep waters of the Caribbean an urn with the ashes of a deceased shipmate of the captain. The officers were all on deck, dressed in clean khakis and the captain in a white uniform for the occasion. The urn was placed on a plank that reached out over the rail, and an American flag was spread over it during the ceremony. Captain Smith read some Bible verses and a poem sent by the widow, and then it was time to let the urn drop. The flag was raised, the board tilted, and the urn dropped into the sea with a splash of finality. Farewell to an old shipmate. . . .

I awoke early the next morning and found we were entering the harbor at Santa Marta, Colombia. Fortunately, it was a beautiful location, for we had to remain with the ship at anchor out in the harbor for five days because all the dock space was occupied by other ships.

Off to port side we had a fine view of El Morro, a castlelike island fortress standing guard over the harbor in the sparkling sea. Nearer to the ship, to starboard as we rode at anchor, was a sandy beach. Behind the beach loomed a protecting mountain, topped by the ruins of an ancient fortress silhouetted against the sky. We learned that beyond the fence at the inland end of the beach was a modern military encampment.

The first day, after sundown, as we sat in our deck chairs gazing over at that beach, we saw a large light come on suddenly, and then another perhaps twenty feet away from the first. They blinked two or three times and then we saw them no more. Darkness prevented our seeing details of what was going on over there or who was on the beach.

One of our male passengers said, "I've been reading a book about a guy in the drug trade called Blackie. Maybe that's Blackie signaling for a pickup!" We laughed at the time, thinking the idea too farfetched.

While we remained anchored in that lovely harbor, the mystery lights reappeared twice more. During the day, there was no evidence to explain the lights — only a stretch of sand backed by brush and the mountain range. At night, when the lights blinked, we couldn't see anyone on the beach, although we thought we heard the lapping of oars in the water.

"Blackie's sending his signals again for a drug pickup," we concluded, still thinking it was fantasy. But perhaps we were perceiving the truth, for some months after arriving back home, I read a news item about Santa Marta's being notorious for just that kind of activity.

On our second day in the harbor, Captain Smith arranged for a launch to take the restless crew members and willing passengers to Santa Marta, a city of about 200,000 population. On a coastal plain backed by the Sierra Nevada Mountains, it was founded in 1525, and was sure to have an old section that we'd enjoy seeing, and of course irresistible places to buy and mail postcards to friends and family back home.

The gangway had been lowered along the port side of the ship to almost water level when a noisy engine indicated that the launch was arriving. When we could see the craft, our visions of a "launch" were drastically revised. It was a dilapidated old boat, painted a faded red and smelling of oil. Members of the crew boarded a few at a time. After the launch had made three trips to the city dock and back, some of us passengers dared to go down those forty-two steps from the safety of a lower deck of our ship. The most difficult step was when we had to let go of the rail to step over open water onto the launch. Two of our men went first and were assisted to board by a rather unkempt fellow. We women felt safer when our men took over the helping-hand work.

"Watch your step!" they warned us, and each of the three women of our group was helped to take that frightening step. The warning was justified, for there was no deck rail to grasp. Inside the small cabin where we were to sit down, there was a gaping hole in a rotting old floorboard. And so I went a-launching with Ottilia and Charles, the couple from New York, and Shirley and George from Detroit.

After reaching the dock in a cloud of oily smoke, we walked about through the old city. Shirley and George invited me to join them in further exploration. We stopped for a Coke after exchanging our dollars for Colombian pesos, buying postage stamps and postcards, and seeing most of the city center. George said he wanted to find a telephone to call his brother in Detroit. Then he'd like to find a supermarket where he could buy some good Colombian coffee to take home.

He found a public telephone quite soon and tried, without success, to complete his call. (This was George's pursuit wherever we stopped, and it did not become an accomplishment until we were in U.S. managed Panama!) Nearby were two small grocery stores, but George was not satisfied to buy their coffee for some reason. In the meantime, we had bought copies of a book about Santa Marta, with a map of the city included.

"Here's a supermarket," George said, pointing to a marked rectangle on the map. " 'Mercado' means 'market.' " It was several blocks distant and George, a fast walker, set the pace while Shirley and I trailed behind him. "Mercado" turned out to be an outdoor market of some kind and definitely not what George had in mind. It was manned by rough-looking men standing around rows of stands. Shirley and I picked our way over the muddy ground between the rows, and George was soon quite some distance ahead of us.

Soon we noticed that we were being stared at by the men standing around. Obviously, this was not a place for women, especially American women in slacks, who stood out anywhere in Santa Marta. There was so little open space in which to walk, and so many men milling about, that we had to walk single file, with Shirley behind me.

"Hold your purse tight," I said to her over my shoulder. I had noticed one of the men eyeing us intently. Now he was coming nearer.

The man brushed past me, and I saw he was sidling up to Shirley. "Walk faster," I urged her. "Let's catch up to George!" He was about fifty feet ahead of us, near the far end of the marketplace. We almost ran to catch up with him. The man dropped back only when we caught up with George, who hadn't even noticed that we might be in trouble. You can imagine what his wife and I had to say to him as we left his "supermarket"!

The next day, we decided to forego the launch transport and amuse ourselves on board the ship until we were anchored at the dock, but after two more days, George, Shirley, and I went ashore again for a taxi excursion to the new tourist area outside the city, the Rodadero. It was on a lovely beach, with tall coconut palms here and there and other tropical trees for shade. For refreshment, one could buy a coconut, split by the vendor with his machete as we watched. Strangely, we were the only North American tourists in that lovely resort area.

On Friday we moved to the dock. When the unloading and loading were going smoothly, the captain rewarded us for our patience.

"I'll rent a bus and we'll go up the mountain tomorrow to a coffee plantation for a picnic," he told us.

Saturday morning at nine o'clock, we were all off the ship and ready to go. The chef had packed two big hampers with picnic supplies, and there was also a large cooler with ice and cans of Coke, all ready to be put on the bus.

There were two men on board the bus that finally drove up, the driver and another much more talkative one, who, we were told, was Carlos, the bus owner. When all the picnic equipment was on board, we ten passengers piled in. Immediately, we were struck by a special feature of this bus: It had a string of brightly colored, obviously home-crocheted, medallions and scallops strung along the top of the windshield. This was the first of our many South American buses with such decoration.

Captain Smith, in a bright red jumpsuit, took the seat beside the driver. Carlos had disappeared, for the first of several times during the day. (He reappeared at intervals, each time with somewhat stronger evidence of stops at bars.) Two of the other men from the ship, and a South American woman who was a friend of the captain also joined us, making fourteen passengers. The captain got up after a minute or so and walked to the rear, obviously looking for something. Then in Spanish, in which he was fluent, he called to the driver. We saw the driver looking for traffic and then turning the bus back the way we had come.

"We forgot to pick up the grill and the hamburger for our cookout. We have to go back to the dock," Captain Smith explained as he returned to his seat.

So back we went. Carlos reappeared and boarded the bus while we waited. It was ten-thirty by the time we were finally reassembled and on the way up the mountain road. At the edge of town, Carlos left us to visit a roadside bar, just before the bus began its ascent of the Sierra Santa Marta.

What a road it was! The bus swung around one hairpin turn after another. The gravel road was so narrow in many places that we all held our breath lest another vehicle would come toward us. Halfway to our destination was the village of Minca, where we made a rest stop. Beyond Minca the road was less traveled and even narrower. Sometimes we'd reach a place where rains had washed away part of the gravel surface. The driver would hesitate, check the possibilities, and then pull as far from the rim of the mountain as he could before proceeding cautiously onward. He was a careful driver, unlike some of the Latin Americans who were our chauffeurs on later expeditions.

Finally the bus drove into a cleared area on a fairly level knoll high on the mountain. It was reached by a one-lane road that ended at an entrance lane between two elaborate gateposts, with a stone saint atop one of them. Views of the surrounding high peaks abounded from the clearing. We had reached our destination.

Perhaps you've seen TV coffee ads featuring "Juan Valdez" on a mountainside with his burro and his sack of coffee beans. That mountainside is exactly what the coffee plantation looked like! Juan could have appeared at any moment . . . there were no cultivated rows of coffee trees (really bushes) on Sierra Santa Marta. The owner's home was a long, low, tile-roofed plaster building. Smaller outbuildings, including a rustic retreat for priests, were nearby. Wooden folding chairs and a couple of tables were set out for us at some distance from the house, and soon our purser was burning charcoal in the portable grill.

There was an abundance of brilliant tropical flowers, mostly scarlet, but what I remember best about the grounds are the pink chickens! Yes, three chickens strutting about among those of ordinary white or red-brown coloration were definitely pink — a tint much like the pink of roses. And I have a photograph to prove it.

The whole day was terrific, thanks to that very unusual and kind freighter captain. It included a tour of a Colombian national seashore park, unlike any in the United States, with domestic cattle roaming about freely and a coconut vendor picking up his stock in trade, newly fallen from the palms. We also had a return trip to the Rodadero tourist area, and a drive to a restaurant for our supper.

Near day's end, there were a few minutes that terrified our passenger group. We were about to descend the last miles of mountain road — a challenge for even our experienced driver — when the bus pulled over for some minor mechanical problem. Captain Smith and the other crew members from the *Delta Venezuela* were outside the bus helping in the emergency when Carlos, staggering from his day of imbibing, got in and sat in the driver's seat. When the repair was made and the driver returned, Carlos declared his right as the owner to drive. You should have heard the shrieks from the passengers! But Captain

91

Smith came to the rescue. He bodily removed Carlos long enough for the driver to take his proper place at the wheel.

Yes, a day to remember, from start to finish. After fourteen years and several voyages on other freighters, it remains vivid in my memory, our visit to "Juan Valdez's" coffee plantation in Colombia.

How could I possibly have imagined all that would happen, all that I would see, all that I would learn, on that wonderful first freighter voyage?

Discovering *TravLtips* at my brother's home had given birth to the idea of going on this kind of adventure, an idea that I nurtured by writing for a subscription. Soon it was not just a whim but a persistent desire. When a desire is persistent, and its purpose is good, I believe it can make a positive difference in a person's life and should be given serious consideration.

When something happens that gives us a nudge toward doing something about that persistent idea or desire, it means that opportunity is knocking at the door. That knocking shouldn't be ignored. It's time to take action, to begin planning. We shouldn't turn our back on the idea, thinking, *Oh, well, it would be fun to do, but maybe. . . .* And then we let ourselves think of all the "what ifs" that arouse fears.

In my own case, the "what ifs" could be (and were, to some extent): *What if no one will talk to me and I'll be all by myself all the time? What if a terrible accident happens — and I break my leg? Or what if I'm robbed in New York on the way? Or I get sick on the ship?*

Those "what ifs" can be deadly. They can kill off an opportunity to act upon our persistent desires and block a basically sound plan before it has come through the doorway to enhance the dreamer's life. The negative "what ifs" can snuff out the flame that could have lighted the way to a most wonderful and life-enriching adventure.

Of course we need to look at the "what ifs" seriously. They may be possibilities — but are they also *probabilities?* To let our persistent desires be blocked by unpleasant but unlikely possibilities is to allow fear to take the adventure out of our lives. However, if our fears persist, we, of an age to know ourselves well, should follow our spiritual compass in making a final decision as to whether something is truly good for us.

Yes, we should be sensible — but not *too* sensible. Otherwise, life will slip through our fingers and one day that persistent desire will fade into the category of "I wish I could have. . . ." Then we'll look back with regret because we didn't take the opportunity when it presented itself. *When Opportunity knocks persistently, answer the door — and invite her in!*

I see my voyage on the *Delta Venezuela*, taken in the heyday of freighter travel, before all-container shipping reduced time in ports, as a highlight of my life and a door opener to other opportunities. Even though I had to "dance alone," it was worth the risk of any "what ifs" involved. It led to priceless experiences, including personal and professional growth and lasting friendships formed on that adventure. *Priceless* is what this cruise was destined to be for me, an invaluable experience in terms of how it affected my future.

It was an uplifting experience, and I'll never regret answering opportunity's knock. "Come dance with us to South American rhythms," it said. And I did.

CROSSING THE EQUATORS OF THE MIND

Lifetime Treasures Are at Our Fingertips

When the long-anticipated special feature of our *Delta Venezuela* voyage was about to take place, I was sound asleep in my cabin. But I came awake with amazing alacrity when the purser called from out in the corridor, "We're entering the Gatun Locks!"

Sleep was postponed! I put on my shoes, donned my raincoat over my pajamas, and went out to the deck where all the passengers gathered. Our ship had joined a line of ships early in the evening, awaiting lock space, much as airplanes line up for takeoff. Darkness was falling when an official Panama Canal pilot boarded and we were allowed to move from the Atlantic Ocean through a break-water into a bay, seven miles from the first Gatun Lock. Progress was so slow that we passengers had gone to bed — but only after the purser had agreed to wake us when we reached the locks so that we could be on deck to watch.

It was almost a week since we'd left Santa Marta. Lasting memories of those days include the muddy water of the Magdalena River, in which we docked for industrial Barranquilla, and our visit to historic Cartagena, where, in the depths of tunnels, early settlers hid from Blackbeard the Pirate.

In this interesting city that reached back to the early Spanish conquest, I also had my first view of a three-toed sloth. Outside a monastery, a teenage boy had one on display — as uncute an animal as you can imagine. For twenty-five cents, the boy let me take a picture.

In contrast, en route to Colon, Panama Canal Zone, we were delighted by the graceful dances of a group of six dolphins, as lovely as any staged ballet. Even the day of waiting our turn to enter the canal was interesting, for we had time to take the railroad train from Colon across the isthmus to Balboa and back again. On this ride, we passed many United States government buildings, including the barracks where, no doubt, a few soldiers awaited eagerly the delivery of their automobiles, still in our ship's holds.

Now, gathered along the deck rails, we passengers watched the lock gates close behind us and saw that we were in the bottom of a huge "box" with windowless walls. Then we discovered we were slowly rising as water flowed into the lock, beginning the climb of this huge ship to eighty-five feet above sea level to Gatun Lake. It would be done in three steps. Gatun was an impoundment, an artificial lake created by the damming of a mountainside river, the Chagres.

In the locks, ships are towed by "mules," sturdy locomotives that run on sloped tracks alongside the canal. The *DV*, finally at the top of the first lock, was hooked by cables to a team of four mules and pulled carefully past a pair of open gates into the second lock. Filled to the same level as the one we had left, the second lock was deep enough to keep us afloat.

The same set of mules towed the ship through the series, climbing the section of curved track to the next lock, like the cable cars climb the hills in San Francisco. As we left the third lock, our engines were activated and we entered Gatun Lake. Under our own power again, we moved out of the traffic lane and dropped anchor to one side in the lake, there to stay until daylight. Back to bed we went for a few hours of sleep.

When I went out to the deck in the morning, an unusual vessel was moving slowly on the lake, going toward the locks. It looked like a passenger ship without windows or portholes, and was painted white. Through binoculars, we could see that its home port was Tokyo, but its name was *Canadian Highway*. This ship, in 1979, was an early "roll on, roll off" freighter, built for the sole purpose of bringing Japanese automobiles to North America. A portent of things to come!

Of course, I was among the passengers on deck for the entire five-hour progression to Balboa and Panama City at the Pacific Ocean end. We didn't dawdle over breakfast and lunch at all, for fear of missing something.

I found the progression through the canal of great interest, for I had read not only of its construction and the difficulties encountered, but also the journals of Bayard Taylor, the reporter who was sent by Horace Mann in 1849 to write about the '49ers in those Gold Rush days, long before the canal was even begun.

Taylor's assignment was to go by ship to the village of Chagres, Panama. From there, native guides would accompany him and other travelers. They would go by canoe as far up the Chagres River as was practical. A mountain spine runs the length of the Isthmus of Panama, and getting over that spine through jungle growth, up slopes and down, was usually done on the back of a sturdy little horse. Eventually, muddy, scratched, and desperately in need of fresh clothes, Taylor reached the Pacific coast, where one of the new United States mailboats took him on the rest of his voyage to California's Golden Gate Harbor. Reading of his hardships made me more appreciative of how much the canal was needed.

Gatun Lake, where we spent several hours, was formed by a dam in the upper Chagres to hold the water back. When our canal pilot took us on the way again, crossing the seven-mile-long lake, we traveled above the channel that had been the bed of the old Chagres River, skirting islands that had once been mountaintops. We left the old river channel to enter water that had filled the bottom of a deep cut, a split in the spine of the mountains that Taylor crossed so laboriously in 1849. Now the water made an eight-mile passage between mountain walls known as the Gaillard Cut. To either side, the mountains rose. Manmade terrace upon terrace widened the gap to an expanse of open sky. It took Herculean labor to complete that cut, easing the way from ocean to ocean for generations to come.

At the far end of the cut, the ship began the eighty-five-foot descent to sea level on the Pacific side, via three more locks: first the Pedro Miguel Lock and farther on, near the end of the fifty-mile passage, the pair of Mirafloras Locks.

We stopped long enough to unload the long-awaited automobiles and other cargo, and soon we were in the Pacific Ocean en route nonstop to Guayaquil, Ecuador, and looking forward to crossing the Equator.

"Have any of you crossed the Equator before?" the purser asked one evening in the lounge.

No one had.

He grinned. "Well, I hope you live through the initiation!" he said with a glint in his eye.

We'd all heard about some kind of a dunking ceremony, and here we were, completely surrounded by water, and at the mercy of our crew!

"How will we know when we're crossing the Equator?" one of the passengers asked.

"From the sign on the line in the ocean," the purser joked, and then said seriously, "We'll be watching, and we'll give a good blast on the ship's horn."

The morning when we were almost there, we

all waited up on the bridge deck to cross the 0° latitude line. The horn's big black steel mouth was within ten feet of where we stood leaning on the rail and watching the sea below. When its loud blast came, we nearly jumped over the rail! Our grade-school geography lessons about the Equator's being at the middle of the torrid zone had led us to expect a heat wave. Strangely, it was cooler that day, and we needed sweaters.

In the evening, the ship's officers held an initiation ceremony. Each of us was blindfolded and taken behind a curtain where we had to plunge a hand into partially set gelatin — after listening to a gory fabrication of what it was. Then one of the men disguised as King Neptune read from a colorful parchment: "Neptunus Rex . . . supreme authority over all creatures natural and supernatural, human, piscatorial, crustacean, hydromedusan, cephalopodous, and amphibious found within or upon the surface of the foaming brine . . . proclaims. . . ." The flowery language continued, announcing that we had crossed the Equatorial Line on the thirteenth day of October 1978, and were initiated into the Royal Order of the Trident. The document was signed by *Neptunus Rex*, witnessed by *Davy Jones*, stamped with the *Delta Venezuela* captain's seal, and presented to each of us. Mine certifies my membership after being "duly subjected to those awful tests by which I [Neptunus Rex] judge the worthiness of those aspiring to recognition." (I have another King Neptune proclamation, written in

100

Norwegian, dated *31.08.84* in the European fashion, and certifying that I crossed the *Polarsirkelen* — in other words, the Arctic Circle. This presentation was near Trondheim, Norway, by a King Neptune with a seaweed outfit, and initiation was done, appropriately, with ice water on the nape of the neck of each passenger.)

Our Pacific Ocean ports were for the discharge of the cargo that remained on board and its replacement with tons and tons of bananas and some of those fruits, like overgrown bananas, called plantains — all in the green stages. We became a banana boat at Guayaquil, Ecuador, in the heart of the banana-plantation area. The ship's holds had controls for refrigeration, and hold after hold was filled, each held to the temperature requested by a U.S. buyer.

I've never forgotten the long line of trucks we could see from the ship's decks when we were at Guayaquil. It seemed a never-ending progression, each truck loaded with wooden crates of bananas. Early in the morning a large group of men could be seen down on the dock.

"They are all hoping for jobs loading bananas from the trucks into the ship's holds," we were told.

As unloading time came for each vehicle, these men persevered through a long day of hard labor. A pair of them stood at the open end of the truck bed to place two heavy boxes of bananas on the back of each carrier. Bent over, the men made their way up a temporary ramp from the dock to the side of the ship, where a wide door gave access to one of the temperature-controlled holds. Talk about backbreaking labor! It went on hour after hour, and the men kept working.

In contrast, I also remember that immediately upon our arrival at the dock in New York, those hold doors were opened and moving belts carried the crates into warehouses in a fraction of the time spent bringing them in by manual labor. North American vs. Latin American modes!

I have so many wonderful memories of those last stops before retransiting the canal to head nonstop for New York with our load of bananas. There was the row of sales stalls only about one hundred feet from our ship, tended by men and women who were descendants of the Incas. There we bought inexpensive handwoven woolens, wonderful items for early Christmas shopping. One day we toured the city of Guayaquil, the principal port of Ecuador, at the head of the inlet where we were docked. I also remember the canoes near the ship each day, manned by Ecuadorans scavenging for bits of wood or whatever might be floating in the inlet.

There was little cargo on board other than bananas when we moved out of the picturesque Guayaquil harbor and went northward a short distance to Manta, a much smaller city with a lovely central park. I remember especially when Merritt, one of our men, sat down on a bench and was immediately surrounded by a group of small shoeshine boys. One lucky youngster got the prized permission to shine Merritt's shoes.

On northward to the Pacific side of Colombia, to Buenaventura, from where we took a bus trip to the mountain city of Cali. There, in the downtown park, several scribes sat and typed letters for customers. In contrast to that scene were the modern buildings, even skyscrapers beyond. Then up a mountainside to a monument in a park from which we could look down at the city and also out to the distant horizon over the ocean.

When we left Buenaventura, it was nonstop to New York except for the required pauses for Panama Canal transit. Many ships go through during the night hours, but we on the *Delta Venezuela* had the special treat of daytime passage most of the distance both ways, in full sunshine — excellent for picture taking.

Those memories are lifetime treasures, adventures into a new world and a marvelous learning opportunity. And from that September 22 to October 29, 1978, to now, so many years later, as I sit in recollection of those times and places, I know that I was enriched in ways not measured in money. I was dancing to a piper who has not ceased to enchant me with his piping, and who has since piped me on board several other freighters for more enriching voyages.

Sometimes travelers return from a journey with memories of only the obvious. Little has been added to their appreciation and understanding of the "hows and whys" of their experience in the area visited. The reason? They haven't bothered to prepare for the journey to make it a richer experience through exploring by reading in advance.

My adventure via the Panama Canal was made more meaningful to me because I had read much of the history of that part of the world. I'd read accounts of the Spanish explorers and of the pirates who had sailed the Caribbean. I'd read a biography of Simón Bolivar, "The Liberator" for whom monuments abounded in South America. I'd taken time to learn about the problems that arose during the construction of the Panama Canal and to find out about the hardships faced by travelers to California via the Isthmus of Panama in Gold Rush days.

As a history buff, I had an idea how Caribbean shores must have looked when Columbus's contemporaries viewed them. And I could imagine the amazement on both sides as the Europeans and the native people came face-to-face. What thoughts must have gone through the minds in each group as they met, their vastly different cultures clashing!

In any traveling, even across our hometowns, we may see streets or parks named for local people, and wonder why they were so honored. To delve into local history can be a very interesting project, one that frequently gets the searcher hooked on history. Old newspapers are usually available on microfilm in the local library. Tracking down the details of how any of our towns developed can hold a person's interest for hours at a time — and result in greater interest and pride in the town.

To cross any part of our own country can be so much more enjoyable if we know some of the stories of people who have been there and of the events in which they participated. Often there will be a booklet for sale, written by someone much like you or me. Have you ever thought of writing some of your area's stories? Many retirees have done so, adding to their own pleasure and to the pleasure of others who read their accounts.

A lively curiosity will help each of us make the most of our travel — close to home or to distant places, or even by book or video right in our own living room. A trip to the library is always the start of an exciting journey of discovery!

"HOW SWEET IT IS!"

Taking the High Road

Jackie Gleason, as Ralph Kramden in his early
TV sitcom, "The Honeymooners," had a trade-
mark exclamation: "How sweet it is!" I echo his
joyous phrase when I think of the changes that
have come into the lives of people today, and
especially into the lives of girls growing into
women in the closing years of the twentieth century. How sweet it is!

The world in which I grew up was a different
world for sure! Before World War II, females,
including those just beyond infancy, were expected to accept limitations in their personal lives
— to be "ladylike," as my mother put it, over
and over, to her only daughter. We girls who
liked athletics were told that we shouldn't be out
there playing ball or climbing trees like our brothers. And the way we had to dress made such
activities almost impossible.

Girls, at least city dwellers such as I, had to
wear dresses or skirts and blouses. No slacks,
no jeans, not even for afterschool play. I recall

what a disadvantage skirts were, even though we girls no longer had to wear them down to our ankles, as had been the style for our poor mothers. My dresses were hemmed to reach about two inches below the kneecap.

And what a trial I must have been to my mother! I didn't spend much time playing with dolls, which would have been easy on my clothes. Instead, I loved to roller-skate, which often resulted in a sudden tripping over a crack in the concrete sidewalk. Besides having scabs on my knees all year except in the snows of winter, I know I was very hard on my clothing. For every scab, there was a ruined white cotton stocking.

Sometimes even my dresses were damaged. Often, for example, when I was roller-skating on the sidewalk in front of our house in Milwaukee, our little dog, Brownie, would come running after me. She'd leap up and set her teeth into the skirt of my dress. Brownie would have a really fun ride, flying out behind me as I skated along! But my dress thenceforth had tooth holes in the hem area. Since roller-skating, which I loved, was then acceptable for girls, my mother eventually realized that locking Brownie indoors was the only way to save my dresses.

Everyone accepted as true the saying, "Boys will be boys." Our brothers could try anything, but girls had to be *ladylike*. I preferred my brother's pastimes to playing with dolls, although in an old snapshot of two neighbor girls and me showing off our new Christmas-gift doll buggies,

107

mine is the largest! I was not doll-deprived. But when my brother received a wind-up train for Christmas, I played with it more than he did! And I loved to work with his Erector set. It had lots of metal strips that could be fastened together with small bolts and nuts to construct buildings, doll-sized chairs, bridges, or boxy automobiles.

Yes, to Mother's disappointment, I was a tomboy. My current dictionary defines *tomboy* as a girl "who behaves like a spirited boy," which sounds rather pleasant. But in as recent an edition as the 1954 *Webster's New World Dictionary*, the word *tomboy* meant "a girl who behaves like a boisterous boy; a hoyden." And what was a *hoyden?* "A bold, boisterous girl," derived from an early word for "an awkward man." No wonder my mother strove to make me more "ladylike"!

Do you remember when a favorite taunt for the girl who bent over too far was, "I see London, I see France, I see somebody's underpants"? I remember it well — heard it often — for whenever the boys would let me, I'd play with my brother (fifteen months my senior) and his friends instead of the neighborhood girls. Try climbing a tree in a dress! The taunt would be sure to come if the boys were around.

But it was fun being a tomboy. I especially remember a day when I was seven. I ran around our house with a water pistol, trying to get into target range to pull the trigger and squirt my brother or one of his friends, who were also running around the house, stopping only long enough to refill the pistol from a glass of water placed on a basement windowsill.

Still, I was less restricted than my mother in *her* growing-up years. Born in 1887, she was the eldest of six children. Her two brothers were next in line, ready to pester her and gang up against her anytime. Since they lived in snowy Madison, Wisconsin, surely she must have engaged in snow-ball fights with them, handicapped by dresses and coats down to just above her high-button shoe tops. Her restrictions increased as she grew to-ward adolescence. She had the misfortune to be growing up in the era of the torture of corsets, which must have been truly horrible on a hot summer day. And most women of that era were resigned to many other restrictions.

If we think back to the years of my maternal grandmother's youth, we can see that women were even less privileged then. Grandma May was born in Wisconsin at the close of the Civil War, and when she married in 1886, she and her scant worldly goods were by law the property of her husband, an Irish immigrant who came to America to work on railroad construction. She had many more restrictions than privileges. But she was in-clined to do things for her children ordinarily done by fathers — such as building a primitive type of iceboat for them. She was also expected to milk the family cow, knit all the socks, tend the garden, and see that meals were on the table when Grandpa arrived home from his ten-hour day at the railroad repair shed. In midwinter she also boarded a crew of ice cutters. Of course, she was bringing up her four daughters to accept restrictions, including the physical restriction of wearing a corset and heavy ankle-length dresses and coats as they matured. It's just the way things were, and women had no voice in trying to bring about change.

When I was twelve or thirteen my mother bought me a girl's "corselet," which I hated to wear, and I complied with her wishes only when given strict orders. Through my teens, I remember Mother sitting at her dressing table encased in that stiff, boned garment she wore, even on a hot summer day (and that was before air-conditioning was even invented!).

My own two daughters, growing up during the days of World War II, always wore dresses to school, but playtime was another matter. And look at us now! Seminudity in summer isn't even shocking today. What a long way women have come in only four generations, and I am grateful.

Women were always totally responsible for the labor of child-rearing and household chores, but until I was halfway through grade school, my mother couldn't cast a vote for the president or any other federal political candidate. That also held true for many state and local elections. Women had long been protesting their lack of voice in the government of the United States, and a few, such as Susan B. Anthony, had made it their personal cause in life. She must have been saddened that at the time of her death at eighty-six in 1906 men still had full control of federal elections.

The phrase "women's rights" had not yet become common. It was accepted that no woman need apply for a job considered to be "man's work" (with the exception of a few early Rosie the Riveters in World War I). She certainly couldn't expect to earn the same salary as a man for work with comparable responsibilities. As in my own experience, as late as the 1930s, a male teacher could get married and be congratulated as he returned to work, but a woman lost her job automatically when she married. As for today's common expression, "women's lib" — that would have brought a blank stare! "What in the world is a woman's lib? Something next to her liver?"

World War I came to its end just after my seventh birthday, in the fall of 1918. Oddly, there is something liberating about wartime. Major wars seem to be followed by major social changes. In 1920, little less than two years after Armistice Day, the Nineteenth Amendment was passed, giving suffrage to women. However, it barely squeaked by then. The amendment needed thirty-six states for ratification, and it had been ratified by only thirty-five when Tennessee, by *one vote* in its legislature, became the thirty-sixth state. And we are told that the legislator who switched his stand from firmly *against* to *for* the amendment did so only because his mother wrote to him that he certainly should vote in favor — *or else. . . .* Never underestimate the power of a woman!

By the time I was eleven, in 1922, my mother, tired of caring for her long, thick, heavy hair, had it bobbed — the first one on our block in Oak Park, Illinois, to do so. It shocked the whole neighborhood! And we girls were being allowed more freedom of dress. Teenage girls and even grown young women bought World War I surplus uniform pants to wear for ice-skating. We laced the leggings quite snugly and pulled wool socks up over the lacing. It was a practical and warm outfit that allowed girls the freedom to have fun on the ice.

I remember when I was thirteen and on a vacation in the country. How I delighted in having cotton knickers to wear around the farm! In high school, we girls wore gym bloomers for physical education, full ones that bloused out to resemble a skirt. But in my senior year, when I was sixteen, we were delighted to discard the gym bloomers in favor of lined black shorts. Progress!

I was a grown-up young woman when it became stylish to wear the forerunners of slacks for informal occasions — white bell-bottomed pants, patterned after the sailor's uniform but without the buttoned drop front. When I went on a vacation as a young woman of twenty, I had a new type of outfit. It was like a knee-length jumpsuit, and had a button-on skirt to wear when going out in public. Blue jeans? No — unless you happened to be a farm girl and had a pair of denim bib overalls! Denim was strictly for work clothing.

Comfort for women was arriving, however, in

more ways than choice of outer clothing. I have a nomination for "great inventions of the 1920s." I experienced the onset of menstruation about two years prior to the availability of the disposable sanitary napkin. What a relief when Kotex came on the market! No man can appreciate it, I am sure, but that is my nominee for the Great Invention Award. What agony it was to walk sixteen blocks to get home at the end of a day in high school in pre-Kotex years. Now *that* is suffering — a kind no male experienced!

Girls and women today have almost unlimited choices. They are not only free to dress as they please, but they also have a wider choice in their way of life and career. We older women of today also had a choice of careers, as compared to a century earlier, but from a limited list. If we left high school after two years, we could expect to be a domestic or a factory employee, a store clerk, or, at the top of the list, a telephone operator. If we took stenography and typing classes in high school, we could get an office job, with or without graduation, as a "steno." That was what secretaries were called back then. To be a nurse, a teacher, or a librarian meant further study after four years of high school. Only a few young women, probably from richer and less conservative families than mine, stepped out into other fields, to become a "lady doctor" or to do something very daring and even dangerous such as Amelia Earhart did.

As I was finishing high school, it was a foregone

conclusion that I would become an elementary-school teacher. My parents made that decision and I accepted it. I don't recall any discussion on the subject. My brother's college education took precedence over a degree program for me. A two-year teacher-certification program for me also lessened the financial strain on my parents in those years at the start of the Great Depression. It was decided that I would go to a teachers' college in Wisconsin, Mother's home state, for those two years. It would not be the one at Whitewater, where my friend Frances had already completed a year, because there was no women's dormitory there. Stevens Point had Nelson Hall for girls, where I, still quite immature at sixteen, from my parents' viewpoint, would have supervision. It was a settled matter — no further discussion called for.

For both of *my* daughters, on the other hand, four years in college were taken for granted as necessary. Connie chose journalism and Mary trained for teaching. I don't know how much parental preferences entered into their choices — I'll have to ask them sometime.

Even though there are still inequalities for women, especially those in minority groups, those of us who have lived through more than half of the twentieth century are aware that we've taken great strides. The young women of today have an almost unlimited choice of careers, and most of them are included in family decisions. Progress may seem slow to today's young women, but it's faster than in previous generations.

Women are now being voted into or appointed to important positions in the federal government. High time! The caring nature and proven intelligence of women are needed to balance the men's decisions, often made, it seems to me, with little regard for the reactions of citizens. For the good of us all, male and female, women should have an equal voice with men in decision making at the national and also the international levels. When that stage is reached in even the nations where women are still downtrodden, there will finally be the peace on earth that God meant for us to experience, and we'll all have reason to celebrate.

Times have changed indeed . . . and how sweet it is!

What a wide variety of options we women of today have before us, and rightly so. For the young woman still in school, her future is an unwritten book whose pages she'll fill in her chosen way.

And what about choices for those of us who are approaching or already in retirement years? We also are fortunate to be living now instead of even thirty years ago, for our options have widened considerably, in line with rapid technological developments. When our children are gone from home and we'd like to try a change of life-style, there are more options open to us than ever before. We have a choice in how we use our time and energies, even if — or perhaps *especially* if — we are dancing alone.

I enjoy watching the TV weekly drama "Northern Exposure." As I was considering the subject of women's choices for this book, I saw the episode in which Marilyn, the very quiet, self-confident Alaskan Indian woman who is the doctor's receptionist, decides to take a vacation. Her desire is to "have an adventure." Joel, the doctor, tries to make very detailed arrangements to ensure her safety in Seattle, where she has never been. But she just wants to go and do as she pleases. As I watched the episode, I was entirely in sympathy with Marilyn. Sometimes we really need to step out and try something new — "have an adventure," as Marilyn put it.

While Joel fretted and worried about her because she didn't follow his instructions, Marilyn gave no thought to unpleasant "what ifs." She enjoyed herself in perfect confidence of her own safety, moving about the city alone.

Many of us, men as well as women, get that same feeling of wanting to have an adventure. But not all people can trust themselves and their inner guidance enough to follow through, as Marilyn did.

"Oh, I'd love to do something adventurous, or at least different," the person who longs for change might say. "But I just can't do anything to change my life and make it better." So she or he plugs along in the same old rut, wanting to do something different but convinced that a change is impossible.

But we'll never get out of the rut in which we've been plugging along until we have the courage and self-confidence to attempt something new. You may have heard the story of the toad hopping along in the bottom of a deep rut in a muddy country road. He wishes he could get out and see the world beyond those muddy walls. He is convinced he can't jump high enough to make it. One day he looks up and sees another toad hopping along freely on the higher level.

"Come on up here!" the happy toad calls down.

"But I can't jump that high!" the toad in the rut wails, and soon the other toad is out of sight. But a little later the toad above the rut is surprised to hear the toad from the deep rut calling to him. And there he is, hopping happily, out of the rut and on the high, open road.

"I thought you couldn't jump this high!" the second toad says.

"Oh, I couldn't! But a big wagon wheel was coming right behind me!"

Sometimes we need that "big wagon wheel" threatening our complacency to have the courage to try something new, to get to the freer open areas. But if we take a major jump because we are forced into it, we may not be moving toward what we'd really like to do. We aren't using our inner powers to our best advantage.

The jump should start with *right thinking,* knowing that we have the ability to follow any persistent desire to fulfillment. Note the word

117

knowing. "Right thinking" implies having enough faith in God and our inner guidance to feel confident in our plans as we think them through.

So we begin to plan and dream, imagining ourselves doing what we'd truly like to do, and then we begin taking steps toward our goal. And when the time is right, the way to make the dream a reality will come if it is truly right for us. It is possible that something even better is in store.

The amazing truth is that all that positive thinking actually has an influence on what happens in our lives. It draws opportunities toward us. And first thing we know, we're up on that high road, dancing along!

Yes, even if we have lived a long time and are "old" in the eyes of youth, we still have choices. And how sweet it is!

ADD A DASH OF FRIENDSHIP

Sometimes We Can Double Our Fun

There are times when we who are alone in life's dance really need friends — special friends whose thinking and life-style are similar enough to our own for understanding and compatibility. I was fortunate to find a few such friends in a study group I began to attend in the fall of 1974 and still meet with every week.

One of those new friends was Dot, who had further qualifications as a special friend with whom I could share some travel adventures. Dot is seven years younger than I, but we both are physically younger than some of our contemporaries, active, rarely ill, and nonsmokers.

When we met in the fall of 1974 as new members at that study group, we both were recently widowed. For Dot, then fifty-five years old, the loss of her husband was truly a major shock; he was her children's father with whom she had planned for years of enjoyment in their new home near one of our Ozark lakes. But he was killed suddenly in an automobile accident en route home from his work. For me at sixty-three, the life-style change was not as drastic. The death of my husband, Howard, from lung cancer had come after a marriage of only three years. While at that time I had financial problems to overcome, I had already learned to dance alone in an earlier decade of being on my own.

A few months after joining that study group, I was about to drive to California, two thousand miles away, when I learned that Dot would like to go with me. This would be a test: Were we compatible enough to share travel accommodations? Several factors are involved in my concept of travel compatibility, especially when the two people will be traveling by automobile and, therefore, together nearly one hundred percent of the time. Similar sleeping and waking habits are very important. Both people should be capable drivers and accustomed to the type of car being driven so that driving can be shared. A similar financial status is also helpful so that both are likely to agree upon motel costs and other expenses. Neither should be a pouter or a griper when a temporary problem arises, but should take a practical and optimistic view of finding a solution.

Before that California trip, another factor was also on my mind. Would Dot be willing to take the little side trips that make traveling much more interesting? Did she have a sense of adventure? I learned a great deal about her on that first long drive. Yes, she was adventurous — not like Harold of that Caribbean voyage, who had been afraid to try something that didn't come with an absolute guarantee of safety!

As we started back from California, the two of us planned to go up in a hot-air balloon at Albuquerque, but were disappointed when weather conditions foiled our plan. That is one adventure we have yet to fulfill. Yes, we're both older now, but we have a mutual friend, older than Dot by four years, who, at seventy-seven, tried hang-gliding at her son's urging and loved it! "Old dogs" *can* learn new tricks!

"Would you like to go with me on a tour of the British Isles?" I asked Dot in the summer of 1981. Our friendship had grown steadily in the intervening seven years. We discussed the cost, and since the dollar was doing well against the British pound, we could each manage it. So off we went in late August, flying nonstop from St. Louis to London, where we would join a bus tour.

It was a great trip, planned for moderate costs through the use of older, less fashionable hotels. We toured briefly in London before the bus took us to Cambridge, to York, and on to Scotland.

Both Dot and I fell in love with Scotland, where our major stops were in Edinburgh and Inverness before we headed westward to famed Loch Ness. (Yes, I think there really is a Nessie down in the depths of that gorgeous lake!) Our last night in Scotland was at Oban, a small city on the western coast.

When I recently asked Dot what was her most

vivid memory of that splendid tour, she said, "Oban." We had both loved that city on the Firth of Lorne, grown from a little fishing port but retaining the Old World feel.

Our hotel, in the heart of the town, and just oozing with atmosphere, was probably the first hotel built in the area. And of all our rooms on that tour, the one we shared in Oban was our favorite. We reached it by a narrow stairway up from the third (top) floor, and found this delightfully cozy place under the eaves. In a dormer there were cushioned chairs, like a window seat, beneath a casement window that opened out to the roof where pigeons cooed. We opened the window and could breathe the sea air, touch the slate shingles of the roof, and almost stroke the pigeons. We felt we were back in the Old World. Off to the left below was the harbor where fishing boats were docking even as we watched.

Another never-to-be-forgotten Scottish highlight was the humped one-lane bridge, over a small river north of Edinburgh, where the bus could not cross with both passengers and luggage aboard. The combined weight would leave the bus stranded at the top of the hump, with all wheels suspended. Since luggage can't walk, we all got out and betook ourselves to the other side of the ancient bridge. There we cheered the bus driver as he safely proceeded over the hump and onto the two-lane highway where we waited.

As we traveled in Scotland, I was enchanted by the fields of heather in bloom, but I became curious about fields of other bushes.

"Are those raspberry bushes?" I asked Linda, our English tour guide.

"Yes, they are raspberries," Linda replied in her refined, soft English accent. "Rahss'bries" was how it sounded to me.

Our Scottish bus driver exploded! "Raazzzberries! Razzberries!" My Midwestern pronunciation came back at me, with the accent on "razz" in a way I've never forgotten!

Heading southward in England again, before going to Wales, we sampled "fish 'n' chips" for lunch one day, eating them on a beach as we sat looking out over Colwyn Bay. We were charmed by the peaceful village of Windemere in the Lake Country. Then came embarrassment on a Sunday afternoon in Chester, when we inadvertently entered an English tearoom thinking it was the equivalent of an American hotel coffee shop. What an error! There we were in our tourist garb, in a room with small tables on which were fine china plates of dainty sandwiches, served with tea to true British ladies and gentlemen by elderly maids in their little white aprons over black dresses. Oh, those crude Americans!

In Wales, after we had visited that old settlement of *Llanfairpwllgwyngyllgogerychwyrndrobwllllantysiliogogogoch* (translation: *Mary's church by the white hazel pool near the fierce whirlpool, with the Church of Tysilio by the Red Cave*), we passed an encampment of local people "on holiday" with their bright-hued plastic tents pitched on a mountainside. A sudden downpour had just ended and the late-afternoon sun had burst through. The people were wringing out towels and clothing as our bus went past. Temporary waterfalls streamed down the mountain into the flooded creek at its base.

Our century-old hotel was just a short distance farther along the road, and we reached it at dusk. As was customary, Linda went in to check on room assignments.

"I'm sorry, ladies and gentlemen," she said upon her return to the bus. "The storm knocked out the electricity, and there'll be a few delays in service. But we can go in." She read off the room-number assignments, and we went into the lobby.

We carried lighted candles as we made our way through the twisting and turning windowless corridors to find our rooms. Spooky! The power came on after a half hour and the cooks could prepare supper for us starving travelers. As we went to the dining room, those same corridors, well lighted, were not nearly as interesting.

We were ferried, bus and all, across the Irish Sea to Dublin. Even more clearly than some of the historic buildings we toured, I recall the residences along the thoroughfare, with their brightly painted front doors, highly polished brass hardware, and decorative semicircular windowpanes. But how incongruous to find in that old Irish city the intrusion of a McDonald's and a Burger King (with WHOPPER in large letters on the window) in the downtown shopping center!

We visited Killarney and Limerick, of course, and we climbed up to the top of the tower in Blarney Castle. A bit of drizzle was going on up there — Ireland owes its green to lots of that kind of weather — but a man was ready to assist us in kissing the famed Blarney Stone, which you have to do while lying on your back, with your upper body over a hole in the floor. The vertical stone is part of the wall below floor level, and to kiss it you must trust the guide to support your back. The stone was black and greasy looking (from lots of lipstick, we were told) and kissing it was not in the least appealing to Dot and me. We decided to blow it a kiss and skip the performance. So what you are reading in this book is "no Blarney"!

I had found a fine traveling companion, I decided. So Dot and I, a year or two after that pleasant tour, made a six-week journey by car to visit the spectacular national parks of the western United States. Our great adventure on that trip, the year after the Mount Saint Helens eruption, was to fly in a small plane from Olympia, Washington, to see the devastation. The pilot, a young woman, confident and capable like many of her generation, took us over the forests that now looked like a giant game of jackstraws and then circled the crater while Dot and I snapped pictures. We went around the mountain a little closer and we kept on snapping. And then again and again — and both of us ran out of film before the final circuit, which took us almost inside the crater.

We flew to London again in 1984, but this time to ferry across the English Channel with another bus tour to spend a week or ten days in Switzerland. That was glorious! We were lodged in a former health resort in Davos. Converted to a ski resort in winter months, it was well up on a mountainside and reached by a funicular. We had a balcony on which we lounged for a happy hour each evening before dinner, gazing at that gorgeous landscape, each of us in a cushioned chaise longue. Who could ask for anything more?

True to her adventurous nature, Dot shared a little two-person "gondola" with me to go to the top of the mountain. There we were, just the two of us, suspended high above the rocky slope in that little cage, swaying as we went ever higher above the tree line. Finally, when we were about to collide with the mountaintop, we came to an abrupt stop inside a shed.

Following that stay in the Swiss Alps and our return to London, Dot and I took the train to York. We spent a day or two there before going up to Newcastle to board the overnight ferry to Bergen, Norway. There, after a Sunday tour out to the beautiful home of famed composer Edvard Grieg, we boarded the Coastal Express cargo and passenger boat for a trip among the fjords and fishing villages.

We went clear around the top of the peninsula

to North Cape and on to Kirkenes, at the Russian border. A short bus trip took us to the fenced boundary line. From where the bus stopped, near the fence, we could see a Soviet military guard post. This was during the Cold War, and on the Norwegian side of the barrier fence, apparently at Soviet insistence, a concrete block had been set into the ground with footstep marks and a camera silhouette painted on it — all pointing at right angles to the fence. We were not supposed to photograph that Soviet outpost. Nevertheless, I have a picture of the concrete block — and one of the ill-fated U.S.S.R.

It was en route to North Cape that I crossed the Arctic Circle and received the certificate in Norwegian that I mentioned earlier. My friend Dot shared that adventure and others. But we are still watching for the right opportunity to go up in that hot-air balloon!

I've been to the British Isles twice since that trip with Dot. The memories that stand out among those from all the journeys are not usually of the tour features in the brochures. They are of minor sights and happenings that make traveling special. Extra-special when you have a good friend to share it with.

But when no good friend is able to go with us, we need not give up on plans to travel. There are special tours planned for people of retirement age, tours that make provisions for those traveling as a single. If you are not yet sixty and eligible for such tours, going alone is not really a problem if you join a group tour traveling by bus. You are quite sure to find another single person — and if not, a friendly pair, as happened to me over and over again.

But if you have reached the age of sixty, there is a travel plan strictly for you, one used by so many single persons that the agency will even try to match your needs with those of another single person to be your roommate. This will save you the cost of the single supplement that most travel plans still require when you ask for a room alone.

When Dot and I made our second European jaunt, that Switzerland vacation, it was arranged through Saga, the travel agency for the person who is sixty or older. Saga's tour packages, expanded tremendously since the time of our trip, are planned to cover air fare and all other costs except personal-choice special items or nontour expeditions. Representatives meet the travelers at the airport and the traveler's next responsibility is settling into the hotel room or ship's cabin already reserved. Luggage handling, insurance coverage — every detail is attended to. And should you request it, Saga will do its best to find a suitable roommate for you. So many singles use Saga as a travel agent that you won't be alone unless you so choose. (Information on how to reach Saga is in the appendix to this book.)

So happy traveling and lasting friendships to you!

NEW FOUNTAINS OF YOUTH

The <u>Real</u> Secret of Staying Young

Picture a kind of Santa Claus version of a hippie, backpack and all, trying to hitch a ride on a seemingly endless dusty road in eastern Australia in the 1960s. That's Marty Knowlton, and he's not having much luck until, finally, one of the cars that appear at long intervals stops at the roadside.

Marty is surprised when he sees that the driver who risked stopping for him is a woman alone. She stares straight ahead, her hands gripping the steering wheel, as Marty tosses his backpack into the backseat and gets in to share the front seat.

"You know, I've never done this before," she says as she puts the car into gear and they start forward. "But I thought you looked so old you wouldn't be a danger to anyone."

Obviously, before stopping the car, the kind Australian woman hadn't seen the youthful grin and lively eyes of this "nondangerous" man with the prematurely white hair and beard. Knowlton delights in telling this anecdote because he considers himself "dangerous" to the aging individual

129

who thinks life's fun and learning ability end at age sixty.

After more months of global wandering, Knowlton accepted a position as a counselor to students at Boston University in 1969. There he met David Bianco, director of student residential facilities. Two men with very different personalities — Knowlton is an unconventional restless wanderer, and Bianco is a more conventional stay-put type — found they were alike in much of their thinking on educational matters. Eventually they would form an alliance from which evolved a plan that would become a new fountain of youth to thousands of people.

But Knowlton's wanderlust soon took him on a four-year backpacking and archaeological-digs tour in Europe. It was 1974 when the two met again, this time at the University of New Hampshire, where Bianco had relocated. They were jointly involved with a youth hostel on campus, and they talked about how much more the young people might have benefited from the experience had they so chosen. In their discussion, Knowlton told Bianco of the folk schools that Scandinavian universities ran for adults who wanted more education.

"Maybe we should be having residential study programs for adults," he added, and went on to express his enthusiasm for the way adults in the folk schools flocked to the universities. Lodging was provided for them in existing residential facilities when the regular students were away. He was most impressed with the eagerness and ability to learn at any age in these people.

Knowlton's experience with adult use of residential buildings in Europe interested Bianco tremendously. After hearing Knowlton's enthusiastic reports, he said, "This campus ought not to be having a youth hostel — it ought to be having an *elder hostel!*"

And in that pronouncement, the seed of Elderhostel — an economical way for older people to combine travel and study — was planted. The seed, watered and nourished over time, would grow into an organized plan of travel and study in almost every area of North America, and indeed the whole world. It has served as a fountain of youth to thousands of people in their later years of life.

Marty Knowlton and David Bianco, with much assistance from Eugene S. Mills, president at that time of the University of New Hampshire, seized on the idea, and the name and plan of Elderhostel came into being. After months of labor, the first courses were offered in 1975. That first Elderhostel was greeted with such enthusiasm that planning for '76 began immediately.

Several basic ideas have prevailed since the first experimental years. An important one was to disprove the stereotypes about older people, summed up in the adage, "You can't teach an old dog new tricks." An arbitrary minimum age was set for participants: The older of the pair of applicants must be at least sixty, and his or her partner cannot be younger than fifty. Original planning also included a stipulation that "hostelships," a kind of scholarship, should be available for worthy persons who couldn't afford the cost but were seriously interested in the short courses offered. Whenever available, housing would be on a college campus, usually during summer vacations for the regular students. The program took off like wildfire, with rapid growth until it encircled the globe, as it does today.

The programs include some of the folk schools in Europe that intrigued Marty Knowlton, and there are a few based on participants residing in homes instead of in campus facilities. In the United States, motel rooms are also reserved occasionally for participants, and there are even a few courses in which the students live on a riverboat or an ocean liner.

And what do the courses cover? Subjects from archaeology to zoology and everything in between. Architecture, ceramics, gardening, history, languages, literature, local cultures, religion, woodcarving — you name it, for the list seems endless. In some of the overseas courses one week is spent in each of a group of three countries, such as Greece, Israel, and Egypt.

A new challenge for Elderhostelers is to participate in a service program, here in the United States or abroad. In the United States the best known is Habitat for Humanity, in which groups of people pitch in to build a new home or renovate an older one for a worthy family (former President

Jimmy Carter and his wife, Rosalynn, are the best-known participants). Seniors have helped reconstruct hurricane-damaged schools as well as homes. Every project is planned for thirteen days, and the cost for room and meals is likely to be from $700 to $800.

Global Volunteers teach and work with people at important tasks in communities in other parts of the world. An example is a three-week session in Indonesia, in which Elderhostelers will teach in a school and help repair and maintain its facilities.

A third organization cooperating in the service program is Oceanic Society Expeditions, for ecology-minded people. Volunteers assist scientists in field observations and data analysis. An example is a two-week study of the endangered pink river dolphins of the Amazon River. Participants live aboard a seventy-six-foot research and excursion vessel. Another study, based in Monterey Bay, California, gathers information on Pacific white-sided dolphins and whales. The "pay" for all of these service projects is the satisfaction of making a difference by serving others.

And now Marty Knowlton wants to see the vibrancy and energy he finds in Elderhostelers put to work "to protect the world for future generations," as Gatekeepers to the Future. Participants in this program learn to think about the world they would leave to unborn generations, and they discuss actions that could be taken to improve that future world.

"It's amazing what a very small group of people can generate," Knowlton says in a recent issue of *Mature Outlook*. "They empower each other intellectually." And, I'm sure, their ideas can be contagious, reaching far beyond the limits of Elderhostel groups.

While Elderhostel was taking root and growing to almost unbelievable dimensions, other ways were also being developed for the increasingly large population of fifty and over who were seeking outlets for their energy. Some in that group even take early retirement for an opportunity to change their lives, perhaps to have more time to devote to hobbies, such as fishing or golfing.

But frequently, especially among people retiring from the workplace, the hobbies lose their allure after a year or two, and the retiree needs something that fulfills the human need to contribute to the good of others. Often, life becomes more meaningful when they find a volunteer activity in which the skills from their former employment prove valuable. Every community needs volunteers in a variety of capacities, and participating in one can boost a person's self-esteem and at the same time help that person find friends with similar interests. And involvement in these renewing occupations can become a fountain of youth for the person who has been bogged down in old life patterns and routines.

A volunteer organization that is tailored for the person who has been successful in the business world is SCORE, the acronym for Service Corps of Retired Executives. It is an association sponsored by our government's Small Business Administration. It is not limited to retirees, but is open to all men and women who wish to help people just beginning a small business or encountering a problem as time goes on. At a SCORE meeting, a new member will often find something else he or she has been missing — friendships.

The ecology movement also offers opportunities for improved living. "In every walk with nature, one receives more than he seeks," wrote John Muir, naturalist, explorer and promoter of the national parks movement. The Sierra Club, dedicated to Muir's ideals, offers many programs, from inner-city projects to repairing trails and facilities in the wilderness. These programs are open to people too young for Elderhostel membership. Another opportunity for growth is with Outward Bound. Both these organizations are included in the resource listings at the end of this book.

Isn't it time you discovered a new spring of the fountain of youth? An inquiry to one of the organizations that interests you may be all you need to find something that will change your life. But it is up to you to take the first step.

While I was writing this chapter, I met with an Elderhostel group on the college campus near my home. There were about forty people present, with youthful eyes and welcoming smiles under those mostly gray heads of hair. They were people who were taking positive steps to keep their minds, bodies, and spirits healthy. They were living actively, and drinking from the waters of the fountain of youth.

There were married couples among them, and also many people who were dancing alone. But there was no one present who was friendless, none playing the wallflower role. In all likelihood, some of the "alones" had come without knowing any of the others, but as I left the room where they were assembling for another lesson (on analyzing handwriting in this case), everyone was engaged in friendly chatter. Ordinary folks, but special in their liveliness of expression and definitely enjoying their dance of life.

It is very likely that many of them had discovered first the fountain of youth that is God-given to each of us. It is part of the standard equipment we're born with, but sometimes it deteriorates for lack of use. That inborn fountain of youth springs from the optimistic frame of mind that accepts God's promise of a fulfilling life, that looks for and sees the probabilities of good.

Youth is not a chronological category, measured in terms of years since birth. I have met people whose youth is left behind before they reach the age of twenty-five. Remember Harold of my day in Caracas, Venezuela? He was in his thirties and already old!

It is truly remarkable how a person's thinking patterns can keep her or him well physically and mentally. Have you ever noticed how some people seem always to be down with an illness and others seem never to have a sick day? It may be partly their genetic makeup, of course, but frequently those who are often sick live in expectation of catching cold or "catching" something worse and are usually worriers.

A young woman was seriously injured in an accident and told she would never be able to walk again. She did not accept that unpleasant verdict and made a recovery so complete that in a few years she was not only walking but also running in a marathon! Such is the power of the mind when combined with attention to the rules of healthful living and to the guiding spirit that dwells in each of us. And we've all read accounts of people in their nineties still participating in marathons. You can be sure *they* are "drinking of the fountain of youth."

The pattern of expecting good to come if we do our part, of following the spiritual guidance God gives us all, usually leads to a joyous life. This is the true fountain of youth — the secret of being young at any age.

HAVE YOU BEEN TO UCLUELET LATELY?

So Many Ways to Brighten Our Lives

We can't all love the same musical tempos. Hard rock reaches the ears of some as pure delight, but drives many others to turn it off — quickly! It's that way with one's concept of great adventures too.

When my friend Dot and I toured the Northwest by car in the summer of 1982, the whole trip was, for both of us, a great adventure. Just seeing a portion of the spectacular beauties of this continent was a treat. The farthest point northwest that we reached before heading south and then eastward was Ucluelet on Vancouver Island, British Columbia, Canada. What? You never heard of Ucluelet?

Many visitors to Vancouver Island are satisfied to visit the city of Victoria, a bit of England in North America at the southeastern tip of the island, and from there to travel to the beautiful Butchart Gardens not far away. But we reserved those attractions for after we'd been to Ucluelet on the Pacific coast.

To get there, we took the ferry from Anacortes, Washington, and skirted the San Juan Islands to Sidney, on Vancouver Island's southeast coast and a few miles north of Victoria. From there we followed the coastal highway northwestward to Nanaimo, famed for its annual motorized old bathtub race to the city of Vancouver. Then we headed inland to Port Alberni, which is at the navigational head of Alberni Inlet, an arm of Barkley Sound, a small bay on the Pacific coast.

"I'd like to see if the boat out to Ucluelet from Port Alberni is still running," I had told Dot. "Do you mind if we take a jaunt up Vancouver Island to see?"

Dot was willing, as she had never been to Vancouver Island before. I had been there about twelve years earlier and remembered with pleasure that boat trip down the inlet. The boat made several stops at small lumber villages, isolated from the rest of the world and dependent upon boats from Port Alberni for mail and supplies. The trip's turnaround was at Ucluelet, a little fishing-port town on the Pacific at the entrance to Barkley Sound. Ucluelet is better known for the amount of fish hauled in and the many seals seen from the bluff on which it stands than for the size of its human population, which is between five and six hundred hardy individuals.

That earlier trip had been on a fine sunshiny day, on board the little mail and passenger boat, the *MV Lady Rose*. In my ignorance of nautical terms at that time, I had asked the captain, a pleasant-faced and gray-haired gentleman, "What does the 'MV' stand for?"

I can still hear his teasing reply as he turned to me with a smile: "Why, the 'Most Virtuous Lady Rose,' of course."

That little boat may be a "Motor Vessel" to him and to other people, but to me she will always be the "Most Virtuous"! I was pleased that she was still operational that September morning, although my teasing captain had retired. But the sun was behind dark clouds as we boarded her, and even before we left the dock, a gentle rain began to fall. We retreated from the small open deck to the passenger cabin, an open room with benches. To one side were stacks of bedrolls and bundles of camping gear, and it soon became apparent that these were the property of a group of eight women, all past their youth (at least in chronological age), and one young man. Each woman dug out a bright-hued rain parka from the gear as the drizzle deepened to a steady downpour that would obviously continue for some time to come.

The rain dulled considerably the scenery, mile after mile of forested bluffs. On my first trip, we had made several stops at picturesque landings for tiny villages that clung to slopes where creek valleys cut into the craggy shoreline. The boat had stopped just long enough to drop off supplies and mail for the lumberjacks. Now a sharp decline in lumbering had eliminated not only most of the stops but also some of the villages themselves.

It bothered me that the wild beauty that I recalled was now shrouded in rain and Dot couldn't see it.

We had gone on down the inlet beyond where it widened to become Barkley Sound when the eight women and the young man made preparations to disembark. They had donned their plastic parkas, and with their gear out on the deck, they stood waiting in the rain for their landing.

The landing turned out to be a "watering," for the "dock" was a raft of about eight by twenty feet, anchored in the water at least 150 feet from an island off to portside. Three canoes tied to the raft awaited to taxi to shore those disembarking. The *MV Lady Rose* slowed, her engines chugging loudly as she approached the raft. By some means I have forgotten, the ship was held alongside while one of the crew dropped a rope ladder and descended to the raft.

Somewhat perilously, with the rain dripping from their hoods, the women and the one man made their way from the *Lady Rose* via the rope ladder. The great pile of gear was handed down, piece by piece, filling all the remaining space on the raft.

The rest of us were out on deck observing the process, glad that the rain had slowed to a drizzle. As we watched, we wondered what was going on in the minds of those eight women, standing on the raft with all their gear. They were obviously about to camp in the rain-soaked woods on the island, which appeared to be uninhabited. We left them huddled together on the raft as the rain renewed itself from its drizzle into a downpour — but they all waved cheerfully as we went on.

Dot and I shuddered at the thought of camping for days on that apparently uninhabited island in the middle of Barkley Sound, with the fall rains to contend with and none of the comforts of home. Not our idea of a desirable adventure, but obviously it appealed to those other women, all not much younger than we were. To each her own!

"How are they ever going to get a campfire started?" I wondered aloud. We envied them not one bit, and we hoped the young man with them was experienced in such a situation.

Despite the chilly rain, the ride through the sound was a unique experience, like peering into a completely different way of life from the North America that Dot and I knew. The expanse of water widened so much that we could see no land off to the south. To the north, when we could see the shore, it was rocky and wooded, and unbroken by settlements. We felt as if we'd taken a voyage to a very strange and very distant land.

When we had gone for some time without seeing a sign of habitation, the boat's whistle blew to announce our approach to a landing at Ucluelet. We could see a small settlement on a bluff, with only the Pacific Ocean beyond, an expanse of gray sea and sky to a dim horizon.

We passengers disembarked and climbed a flight of steps to the top of the bluff where the village of Ucluelet huddled. Fishing was the industry that supported the people of the village, people who lived in isolation on the tip of a finger of land, with water below in three directions. We were welcomed into the warm and dry, bright open room of a store and restaurant. Women were waiting there to take our lunch orders and sell us souvenirs of this special place. And wonder of wonders, when it was time to leave Ucluelet the cloud cover was breaking.

On our return trip to Port Alberni, the women we had left on the raft were watching for us, waiting on a narrow beach on the island, with dense woods behind them. Thankfully, the sun's rays were shining through and picking up the last of the raindrops. As we went by with a toot on our whistle, the women called and waved enthusiastically.

Those were women active in their dance of life! My own adventure of a trip to Ucluelet and back to Port Alberni paled in contrast to theirs. Even our prime adventure of the flight around Mount Saint Helens in Washington seemed far less courageous than the wilderness living of those women.

It is possible that they were engaging in one of the many experiences offered by Outward Bound. This organization, according to the brochure, has programs of "rigorous adventures that develop vision, responsibility and courage" designed for various age groups. Some are only for teens, such as special programs for youths-at-risk (defined as "good kids making bad choices"). Most are for adults, either planned for families, or for couples only, or for young adults seeking challenges. And many are for men and women of any age.

Outward Bound's practice is to state a minimum age, but the maximum is flexible, requiring only that an applicant be "in good physical condition, willing to try new experiences." A few courses are for women only. Some courses have a minimum age of forty or fifty and are less physically demanding than those planned for younger individuals.

Before the outings begin, the students are taught the hows of the physical accomplishment involved, for the safety of those they guide is of paramount importance to the instructors. Then, after guidance through fundamentals, a challenge is offered. It is one that the students are capable of meeting, but in most cases it will require great physical effort. Success in meeting this challenge is sure to increase a student's self-worth and self-confidence.

"The problems did not change while I was gone [to Outward Bound]," wrote a young woman, "but I know I did." A woman of forty-three wrote, "My son will never believe his tired old mother climbed that rock! Glad I have pictures!"

Another organization that sponsors group adventures is the Sierra Club, which is devoted to caring for our natural resources. Once a participant reaches the group's starting point, further travel is by foot, on a bike, in a canoe, or occasionally by van. Many of the outings are service oriented. A group may undertake a preservation project, such as keeping a trail in good condition, refurbishing campsites, mending a bridge, or maintaining archaeological finds. Almost always these projects are away from main highways and in ruggedly beautiful surroundings.

A few Sierra Club outings are in other parts of the world, but basically its activities are in North America. Some trips are moderate in physical activity, more are strenuous. Men or women may apply for all. Acceptance for an outing is based upon the individual's qualifications, determined by a detailed application form. And no radios, sound equipment, or firearms are allowed. Sierra Club is for active people who appreciate our country's natural beauties.

We can enliven and improve our lives in so many ways! Some of these vacation plans may be perfect for people who are feeling dissatisfied with their everyday accomplishments and are looking for ways to find fulfillment.

And there are plenty of choices in these adventures for women as well as for men. Isn't it great that girls as well as boys are now growing up knowing that they have the power to realize their dreams, whatever those dreams may be? The old idea of men being superior to women in meeting challenges is steadily losing credibility. Women can accomplish almost anything for which they have the desire and are willing to make the required effort. In some cases, we may be limited by physical strength and size when compared to men — but definitely not by mental power.

Our dance grows livelier!

SOMETIMES WE MISS A BEAT

But Our Invisible Partner Never Does

If you drive a car, I'm sure that at one time or another you have found yourself in some unplanned difficulty. I've had a few such incidents myself, usually in circumstances where I could blame no one but myself for my error.

When Dot and I were traveling out West, our plan was to see as many of the national parks as we could on a six-week adventure. We were using my car, quite new at the time, and sharing the driving. I usually carry my spare set of keys in a zippered pocket of my purse, but for this trip I turned over the spare set to Dot. We had an understanding that the driver was responsible for seeing that the car was locked — and also for facing up to a traffic-violation charge if stopped by an officer.

Only once on any of our automobile trips were we followed by a car with siren wailing and dome light flashing, that most unwanted sound and sight. It happened on our return trip from that tour of the national parks and the great West, when we were heading east. Dot had the misfortune to be at the wheel.

She had dutifully stayed behind a truck struggling to climb the two-way mountain road to Cloudcroft, New Mexico, with no opportunity to pass safely. We were a bit concerned because a snowstorm was threatening, daylight was almost at an end, and we wanted to get over the mountain and down to a safe place to spend the night.

The highway followed through the little town, on a very wide main street. Dot's only mistake was to gun the engine audibly to get around the truck on that street. But she did it just as we were passing the police station, trying to get by before the street narrowed to highway width. Sure enough, a policeman followed us as we started the descent from the mountain. Dot pulled off the shoulderless road in the first wide area to the right.

"This isn't fair!" I protested. "That was the only place you could pass safely." And I made my ideas known to the officer as well as to Dot. Back we went to Cloudcroft for her to pay the fine.

"You stay in the car," she said to me. "I'm afraid you'll tell them what you think of their speed trap, and I'll get a bigger fine!"

So I waited in the car, brooding over the injustice of it all, and vowing to avoid Cloudcroft in the future. We've driven back from California since then — but never through Cloudcroft!

I couldn't blame Dot for that incident, because

her driving was not at fault. But I *certainly* had to blame myself for what had happened on our westward-bound adventure when we reached the parking area at the south rim of the Grand Canyon. I had been driving when we got out to view the canyon. The moment I closed the door, I realized that the car was locked and my key was in the ignition. Dot's key was also inside the car.

The car had the old type of locking devices, so shaped that a little work with a coat hanger might release the lock. But we had no coat hanger outside of the trunk, which was also locked. Seeing a couple of RVs parked nearby, we reasoned that it was likely there were coat hangers inside the vehicles. We located the owner of one and explained that we'd like to borrow a coat hanger to try to unlock a door of our car.

Within less than two minutes, a contest was on! Not only did the man volunteer to perform the unlocking feat but so did another man with a hanger.

Each man took a side of the car, a two-door model. People turned from viewing the marvels of the Grand Canyon to watch the contest and cheer on the men with the coat hangers. Dot and I cheered the loudest when one of the kind gentlemen produced an unlocked door.

The next time I committed that error was only two or three years ago, but this time it created a much more serious problem. I was driving alone on a research trip, eastbound along the Ohio River. That sunny August day of exploring had begun at the confluence of the Ohio with the Mississippi. From there I'd made frequent stops for historical sites, following the Ohio's north bank as closely as highways would allow.

At half past four I was at the turnoff for a historic site in southern Illinois, the Cave-in-Rock State Park. This was on my list of "must sees." I had enough daylight left to make my stop, but no time to waste, because I wanted to take plenty of pictures.

The cave's history had fascinated me for years. Cave-in-Rock was named for its appearance — a cavern in a rocky bluff on the north bank of the Ohio River. Down through the ages, the waters of the river cut an arched opening about sixty feet wide and thirty feet high in the face of that bluff. No archaeologist knows how long that cave sheltered humans as well as animals, but evidence indicates that it had been in use since prehistoric times. More recently, Indians had used it as a council house until white settlers drove them farther west.

Cave-in-Rock became a place of disrepute as the eighteenth century was drawing to a close. Back then, facing the river at water's edge, a sign announced: *Wilson's Liquor Vault and House of Entertainment.* Unfortunately, Wilson and other abominable characters, such as the murderous Harpe brothers, had evil intentions toward boat crews and pioneer families who stopped in the area. The cave became notorious as the hideout of thieves and murderers. Many a flatboat crew was lured inside and robbed and killed. Then the cargo was taken to New Orleans for the profit of the thieves.

Today the cave is the tourist attraction in a small state park reached via the little town of Cave-in-Rock, Illinois. The afternoon of my visit to the area, I drove through the town and to the parking area for the cave, mindful of the short time of daylight that remained. The sun was dropping low in the sky and I knew that I had better hurry in order to get the photographs I needed for my article.

When I pulled into the paved parking area at the foot of the bluff on the side away from the river, only two other cars were there. I had two cameras to take with me into the cave — my favorite easy-to-use camera with color film and my more complex one with black-and-white film. I covered my purse on the car floor with my large road atlas, took a small camera supply bag, set the electric door locks, and, keys in hand, closed the door.

I saw that I would need to climb up the bluff via steps built for the visitors' convenience. There was a break in the steps halfway up the bluff for an open level that was also available for parking. When I reached that level, I realized that I had not taken my flash attachment for the black-and-white film camera, and I would surely need it inside the cave. So I headed back down to the car and opened the passenger's side door to reach the case with the flash attachment. I had to set my keys down to free my hands to get it. Then, as was my habit, I locked the car door by using the electric-lever control.

I was back up to the midway parking area when the horrible realization came. My keys and my purse were locked in the car! All I had with me were the cameras and supply bag.

I might just as well get on with my visit to the cave, I thought. *I'll face the problem of getting the car unlocked afterward. No use wasting this good sunlight!* So I climbed to the top and then down to the entrance to the cave, about five feet above river level. I met a few people coming up as I went down, but when I reached the last step, no one was in sight.

Strangely, no one else was exploring the cave when I entered it. Over the centuries, a narrow pathway had been worn down about two feet into the rock floor, so that one walked along a narrow passage, perhaps thirty feet, to the great room beyond. The river's frequent flooding had paved that rock-strewn walkway with red clay, which was a bit slippery even on that sunny day. Carefully, I made my way into the cave's depths and headed toward the large room. The room was shadowy and dim in the cave's recesses, but it was partly illuminated by late-afternoon light from an opening in the ceiling off to the right.

Though a state park, this cave was in its natural condition, with no electric lighting, protective rails, or guides. Totally alone, I made my way gingerly along that treacherous passage. I stopped to take a few pictures with each camera, and still no other person was within sight or hearing.

I wanted to go on into that big room, and scan the scratchings on the walls and imagine the presence of the villains who had once been its occupants. But as I drew near the end of the narrow walkway, I felt something that made me shudder inwardly. I knew, of course, of the many murders that had taken place in that high-ceilinged chamber, and it was as if the evil done there, and the agony of the victims, still vibrated against those rock walls.

A thought occurred to me: What if I were to slip and fall? I shuddered. Obviously, all of the day's visitors had departed. No one would be there to help me, and even the most adventurous of people must occasionally have to depend upon others. Someone finding my out-of-state locked car the next morning might think I had committed suicide! Such were the thoughts, combined with the scary atmosphere in the cave, that prompted me to turn back while I could, and I've never ventured back into that abode of evil.

I climbed up the bluff and down on the other side, hoping to find that I had not locked all the doors. Unfortunately, my electric locking system was very efficient. No other cars were in that parking lot, but I had seen some people on the middle level, so I went back up. I needed a ride back to the town of Cave-in-Rock to find a locksmith.

The only people on the middle level were a

couple and their three children, about to leave in a subcompact. It would be a tight fit for another passenger, but I said anyway:

"I've locked myself out of my car and need to get back to Cave-in-Rock to get someone to open it. Could I hitch a ride with you?"

The woman looked at her husband questioningly. It was a little less than a mile, and I could have walked, of course, but the sun was low and time was important.

He looked a little doubtful. The children were already climbing into the backseat and the space left was hardly enough for me to get in too.

"Sure," he said, despite the problems. But just then a red pickup with a man at the wheel pulled alongside the car. The driver spoke to the family man, who seemed to know him. As the lone man was about to drive off, I quickly evaluated my risks and decided he looked like a solid-citizen type.

"Are you going to town?" I asked. "I've locked my keys in my car and I really need a lift to go for help."

Perhaps my guardian angel had guided this obliging, pleasant person my way, for he quickly offered to take me.

"Sure," he said. "Climb in!"

On the drive to town, I asked him if he knew of someone who might be able to help me.

"What you'd better do is go into the store and see if someone there can get you some help," he suggested.

The store was a slightly modernized version of the old-time general store. He stopped in front of it, and I got out with a heartfelt thank you for his kindness.

A woman seemed to be in charge, and a few other people were either buying items or loafing. I talked with the woman about possibilities, but the only person anyone could think of lived miles away and "likely wouldn't be around, anyway."

Finally, the woman in charge suggested that I call the sheriff at the county seat that I had come through about thirteen miles to the west. She nodded to indicate the public phone on the wall next to the entrance door.

"But I have no money for the call," I said. "My purse and everything but my cameras are locked in the car."

"You don't need any money to make the call," the kind woman said, and then told me the number to dial.

A woman answered the sheriff's phone, and I told her my problem. "There's no one on duty now," she said. "One of our men is in the hospital and John has done double shift. He just went home to get some rest and some supper."

"But I don't know what to do. I'm traveling alone and. . . ." My distress was evident. If only I had some money, or at least a credit card! The daylight would soon be gone, and I wondered what I could do for the night. I had passed a small motel about a half mile north of town, but who would give me a room with no credit card or identification of any kind?

My desperation must have touched the woman at the sheriff's office. There was a moment of silence, and then she said, "Call back in about twenty minutes and I'll see what I can find out."

Even though it was the time of year with long daylight, the wait brought darkness twenty minutes closer. Panic began to set in. What if she had been unable to get someone to come to my rescue?

And then, somewhat tardily, I turned to God. *Help me, Father*, I prayed silently.

I dialed the number again.

"Watch for him. He's on the way," was the cheery report. And sure enough, in only a few minutes, the sheriff's deputy, in plain clothes, drove up.

"No problem, I'll get it open for you," he said with confidence. "I've unlocked lots of cars."

"Even a car with electric windows and no button sticking up on the windowsill?" My car didn't even have the standard door handle, just a flat piece in the framework of the upper part of the door and a tiny keyhole beneath it. It was the most burglarproof car I'd ever had.

"Don't worry. We'll get her opened," he assured me.

At the parking area my "Prince" (I'm one of those women who name a car soon after buying it, and this was a prince of a car) was waiting in the evening shadow cast by the riverside bluff. The kind deputy took out his flat plastic tool with a hooked end, and with much effort, forced it over the tightly closed electrically operated window top into the interior of the car. He tried to hook a latch, but this car was designed to foil break-ins. Again and again the hook simply slipped off the small lever on the solid part of the door below the window and didn't budge the latch. The keys were in plain sight on the car seat, but there was no way to get them out even if he hooked them.

A half hour later, with shadows deepening, he had tried each window and then the door latch. No success. Frustration was beginning to take over when a kibitzer arrived and made an attempt, also in vain. Then another car brought the town marshal to check the progress.

He, too, had a tool that could have opened the latch on any car but this one. He got to work on the passenger's side door, and more minutes passed. The men were remarkably controlled. There were no remarks to me about why I had been so foolish, nor were there any audible cusses. As for me, I was praying silently for success.

Finally, my prayer not having been answered yet, and the two men having worked at least a half hour, I said, "I guess I'll have to ask you to break a window."

God or my guardian angel must have been testing everyone's patience. I had no sooner spoken than I heard the angels sing — in the form of the click of a lock release. The man on the passenger's side had somehow managed to get

157

that little lever to come up. I seized the door handle, and never again will the sound of that door's opening be so welcome.

My rescuing knights would accept no money now that I was able to retrieve my purse and offer them a twenty-dollar bill.

"Just glad we got it open and could help you," one of them said.

Before driving to the local motel, I stopped at the store back in town, and after expressing my appreciation, I bought a book about the area written by a local historian. It will always carry special meaning and memories.

When I arrived back home from that trip, one of the first things I did was to write a letter to the editor of the county newspaper, praising their law officers and the kindness of all concerned in Cave-in-Rock. It was published and a copy was sent to me. Nice folks back there.

We frequently hear and read about terrible crimes against total strangers, but we seldom learn of deeds at the other end of the spectrum of human relations, of the many people who work without reward to help others in trouble. The world is full of decent, caring people who devote their lives to helping friends and family and strangers, such as those townsfolk who helped me that evening when I desperately needed to get into my car for my ID, credit cards, and money.

On that same trip, I failed to put away the

credit card that I had just used to sign for a motel room, and I didn't notice that it wasn't in my billfold before I drove away. About three hours later my inner voice began nagging me to be heard, and then suggested I check my wallet for that valuable card.

Aware then that it was missing, I stopped at the next public phone and called the motel where I had last used the card. The pleasant-voiced desk clerk said that someone had picked up my card from the floor and turned it over to her. More kind people! I drove back immediately, of course, and was out only the time and a little gasoline.

On another occasion, I was driving home from a business trip. The sun was low in the sky when, with about one hundred miles still to go, I felt myself in danger of falling asleep at the wheel, something I never have done. I pulled off onto the shoulder of the divided highway, locked the car doors, leaned back, and closed my eyes.

I awoke to darkness and saw that it was almost ten o'clock. I turned on the car lights and tried to start the engine. No sound of response as I turned the ignition key. I tried again and again. Finally I knew I needed help, but this was before I put a two-way radio into my car.

Over the years, I have learned that to have things go as they should, I can get help from God. God watches over me, I am convinced. So, after asking for help, I took my flashlight, got out of the car, and stood with the light shining on me. I continued to pray.

After a very few minutes, a car with a man and woman passed me and then pulled to a stop on the highway shoulder. The man walked back, took my flashlight, and checked to make sure there was no one hiding in my car. He then drove me to the next town and saw to it that a filling-station man he knew would go back with me. More good people! Blessings on them all!

I have a conviction that a person receives the type of treatment that she or he has always given to others. It's the Golden Rule in action. Add to this a faith in God and His troop of guardian angels, and you are always protected!

A SOARING SPIRIT

Every Heart Has Wings

At the start of my last freighter voyage, I was surprised when the chief steward himself took care of my luggage and other needs when I boarded. He was apologetic and a bit distracted because he was without a permanent room steward for the voyage. But if passenger service from the chief steward was unusual, the real surprise was that the room steward who appeared the next morning was a woman. And what an extraordinary young woman she was.

"Jennielouise," she said when I asked her name, and I later learned that it was written as one word. I introduced myself and then asked, "Are you the room steward for the voyage?"

She laughed. "Seems like I am. I just happened to be at the agency yesterday when a call came. So here I am, off on another voyage to somewhere or other!" She spoke with a slight accent that sounded German.

My first impression was that she was quite young, but further acquaintance made me realize that she had experienced more in life than was likely for a person in her early twenties and was probably in her thirties. Her blond hair was cut short for easy care, and she was also short in stature, about five feet tall. But in all else, including wisdom, the adjective *short* would be a mistake.

I thought I'd see her in other clothing at mealtime, because on all my other freighter trips the room steward was also the passengers' meal steward. But I soon learned otherwise. She did not serve the meals, where male waiters seem to be the custom, but worked only at cleaning, assigned to the crew's quarters as well as the passengers' rooms. First thing each morning, I'd be aware of her mopping the corridors on the passenger deck before we passengers were out of our comfortable beds.

Jennielouise was an example of today's young women and the kind of choices open to them. To her, travel by sea was fulfillment in a very special way. She would leave her bunk at four A.M., dressed in her working-day garb — black toreador pants, a long white shirt with sleeves cut off above the elbows, white socks, and tennis shoes. Then out she would go to the deck.

The 650-foot-long cargo liner had a minimum of lights. In the darkness, the ship that had loomed massive at dockside seemed insignificant on the face of the limitless sea. Overhead, the sky was a wonderment, its vastness like a great star-strewn canopy. Jennielouise watched the astronomical

162

bodies in their movement, so ordered and yet so mysterious, and it is not surprising that she believed there were inhabited worlds other than our planet Earth. What greater way of meditation is open to a person than to gaze at the night sky in the midst of the boundless ocean? I am sure that, whatever her concept of God, she was in communication with the Master Intelligence.

For several weeks of that forty-five-day voyage, Jennielouise and I were the only women on board. Her working visits to my quarters each day were a revelation to me. I had never met a young woman like her, and I looked forward to our conversations.

I respected her need for privacy and did not pry into what she chose not to reveal. She told me enough, however, for me to learn that, though she was born in the United States, she had lived in Europe for some of her childhood years, which accounted for her accent. She had tried different life-styles but was basically a loner who must continue to make her own choices. When we parted at journey's end, she had some concerns about her health and had decided not to sign on for another voyage.

I dreamed of a different life-style, she wrote on a postcard she sent me months later. *It seems like travel is my fate in life.* Having attended to her health problems, she was again to be on the open seas. The postmark was Galveston, but she did not give me any address to which I could respond.

My next word from her came a year later on a postcard from Argentina, and this time she included her surname and a temporary return address. I could at last write to her, and did so. She was staying in Buenos Aires for a while, and she planned to study Spanish upon her return to the United States. The next and last card she sent to me was mailed in 1992 from San Francisco, where she was living in a Chinese hotel.

Back in America is wonderful, but I'll go again, she wrote on that last postcard, so I don't know where she is at this moment. There is no likelihood that she'd light for long in San Francisco's Chinatown, and she may well have registered for a voyage from California to who knows what destination. I look forward to hearing from her again.

That last message was written on the back of a postcard depicting a café in San Francisco. According to a caption on the card, the café was not only a gallery and meeting place for local artists, but it also featured a "booth for lady psychiatrists"! Although I'm certainly not a "lady psychiatrist," sometime when I'm visiting my daughter who lives near San Francisco, we'll stop in at this self-styled "Rendezvous for Creative People." Should be interesting — and perhaps they'll remember Jennielouise.

Meeting Jennielouise was an added bonus to my adventure. I see in her today's changing woman, who has visions beyond her daily tasks, and sees her occupation as an opportunity for expansion of her spiritual life. I feel that her work as a steward is only the means to satisfy what she describes as her "peaceful spirit." She may appear to be alone, but she is never a wallflower, for she is a participant in her chosen dance of life, to the tempo in which her inner spirit leads her.

We, too, would do well to let our spirit soar. Spirit can reach far beyond the walls and roof that shelter us, even if we are physically bound to remain within those walls. How does one let the spirit soar? For each of us it may take something different to be the wind under our wings.

For some of us, listening to music may give rise to our spirit, making it soar above our actual surroundings. Or reading a letter from a longtime friend may bring to mind the joys of an old association and so be the means of making our spirit soar. Perhaps we've found a book or even a magazine article that so absorbs us that we are uplifted until we must return to our familiar surroundings. Or maybe we've created something with our hands from raw materials, and our spirit soars as we view it in completion. As a writer, I find that my spirit takes wing when I read or reread a letter inspired by something I have written that was appreciated. And, like William Wordsworth, "My heart leaps up when I behold / A rainbow in the sky. . . ."

Some of us feel such a soaring of spirit when we have done a kindness and see the response in another's eyes. Our spirit may soar when we learn of the wonderful accomplishments of one of our children, or when we hold in our arms a newborn grandchild. Or perhaps our spirit soars when we sit quietly in meditation. Whatever it is that does this for us, we are soothed in body, mind, and soul, as if relaxing in gently lapping warm waters.

Wherever you are, Jennielouise, I salute you and your soaring spirit that knows there is more to life than the mundane and the obvious.

CRISIS CONTROL

Some Lessons in Living

There have been times when my dance of life tempo was flowing in a glissando that broke to a sudden burst of pizzicato — a change that made my heartbeat go into race mode. Such a time occurred when I was alone in Copenhagen a few years ago.

Just before my seventy-sixth birthday, I sailed for Antwerp, Belgium, on the *Otter*, a freighter embarking from Montreal. Upon reaching Antwerp, her home port, cargo was unloaded and the *Otter* went into dry dock.

I was told of this plan about a month before sailing date. Passengers could either cancel their reservations or plan to be off the ship for two weeks, going wherever they chose. My choice was easy.

That's great! I thought. *I can use the railroads to see some of the northern European lands I've missed.* Since a Eurailpass has to be purchased in the United States, I bought a first-class one that would be good for any fifteen-day period

167

and a guidebook for Eurail travel. I hoped that another single passenger would make the same choice, but on this point I had to trust to luck, for I didn't know any of the other passengers. Though it would be more fun if I had a new friend to share the railroad adventure with, I'd use that pass even if I had to go alone.

I did meet a new friend, Shirley, on board the *Otter*, but she had bought a BritRail pass, and the two are not interchangeable. So when we had to leave our comfortable quarters on the *Otter*, we parted in the Antwerp depot to take different trains. I boarded one heading toward what was then West Germany. I carried my rail pass and guidebook in my well-filled purse, a carry-on bag stuffed to zipper-straining point with shoes and minimal changes of clothing, and a tote for my camera, sweaters, snacks, and incidentals. The rest of my travel equipment was back on the ship in a locker.

I had chosen Bremen for my first overnight stop, and it was late afternoon when I arrived there. I quickly located the tourist bureau, exactly where the guidebook said it was.

I told the pleasant English-speaking attendant that I would like a nice, inexpensive room for the night, one that was an easy walk from the depot.

She picked up the phone and a minute later was directing me to a small hotel only two blocks away. Soon I was depositing my carry-on bag and tote in a bright, nicely decorated room. With two hours of daylight remaining, I set out to have supper and then take an evening excursion to the market square near city hall. I had read in my guidebook that a statue representing the Brothers Grimm fairy tale of "The Four Musicians" was there.

The charming statue made me laugh out loud. There were the four bronze animals standing on one another's back. Largest, at the base, was the donkey, topped by the dog, the cat, and the rooster.

Many local people had gathered in the open square. A band and a magician provided entertainment from a platform equipped with an amplifier. I listened and watched with the others, enjoying every minute despite my lack of a companion. Pleasantly tired, I returned to my room for a good night's rest.

It was fortunate that I slept well, for the next evening would be in great contrast. I had decided to go to Copenhagen, where the train would arrive at six P.M. I felt a warm glow as I left Bremen in the early afternoon, for my first venture into this part of Europe had turned out well.

In the last hour before my train arrived in Copenhagen, I studied my guidebook so that I would remember the location of the tourist bureau where I could get a hotel room for the night. I was to detrain at Kobenhavn H, in the heart of the city, directly across the street from Tivoli Gardens. Convenient, I thought, but the gardens would have to wait until the next day. I hoped to find a hotel room within a block or two of the station.

According to my guidebook, the tourist bureau's room-service office was at the far end of the cavernous, arch-ceilinged main hall of the depot, between the police station and the post office. I could identify it by the sign *Kiosk P.*

Getting off the train was always a bit difficult, because there are no waiting porters to assist the passengers. My overfull carry-on bag hung by its strap from my left shoulder and my purse from my right. My tote bag, also stuffed full, was on my left arm, leaving my right hand free to grasp the handrail. With the disembarking achieved, I saw that I was about two city blocks distant from the entrance to the huge station building. My arms were already aching with the weight of my luggage as I entered the great hall. At the far end, as the guidebook had said, there were signs for the post office and police station.

But there was no "room service" sign in any language between them. *It must have been moved,* I thought, and began a search among the many kiosks. Since I had had no supper, I was hungry and growing more tired with each trip around the great hall in my fruitless search for the room-service kiosk. I found a currency exchange where I could get some Danish kroner, including coins I would need for a rest-room stop.

Another circuit of the many kiosks and still no success! My arms ached terribly and I was so tired that tears stung my eyes.

This will never do! I thought, and I headed back to the money kiosk to get the ten coins needed to rent a locker to lighten my load. What a relief to stand up with no weight on my arms! With all but my purse stowed, I bought a snack to give me the strength I needed to go on. Finding an unoccupied bench, I sat down to eat and try to recuperate a bit.

If only I can find someone who speaks English! Room service must be somewhere in or near this depot! Just then, an American young man I had seen on the train approached. Help at last! Yes, he could show me where the elusive kiosk was. Following his directions, I reached the counter. It was in an obscure corner that I must have passed several times.

"All the nearby rooms are gone," the young man behind the barred window told me. He looked at his charts. "I can get you a room at a small hotel about five or six blocks away," he said, and picked up the phone as I nodded assent.

A minute or two later I had paid him the room charge, which would be credited at the hotel. Then he took a small map and marked the hotel's location on it.

"Go out the main door and follow the street to your left," he directed me. "Walk three or four blocks to —— Street [a Danish name], and turn to the left for one block. Then turn right and the hotel is in the middle of the block." He gave me my receipt and the map.

I decided I was too tired to carry my luggage

that far and would leave it in the locker. After stuffing a couple of essentials from my carry-on bag into my purse, I closed the locker and headed for the exit door, map in hand. With just about enough time to reach the hotel before dark, I followed the first street to the left as directed. I had spent about two hours in the depot.

When I had walked four blocks without seeing the street sign where I was to turn left, I began to be concerned. The neighborhood was definitely deteriorating. Railroad tracks on a weedy right-of-way paralleled the street to my left. The clerk had said nothing about crossing the railroad, as I would have to do in making that turn to the left. Dingy old unoccupied store buildings were on my right. Their dirty windows were plastered with ads for beer and faded, lurid posters of semi-nude women.

I walked another block, past more littered doorways and a pornographic movie house. Panic was setting in. In midblock, with the open door of a saloon visible at the next corner, I knew I was in trouble . . . no respectable hotel would be in a neighborhood like this! Surely that room clerk wouldn't send me *here!*

I'm lost! I must be going the wrong way! The realization hit me, and I didn't dare stop to compare those confusing street signs with my map. That would be a signal to those men at the corner that I was vulnerable. I must keep on walking — but where? To that saloon with the open door across the street at the next corner?

Night was coming and I was lost in what was probably the worst section of Copenhagen. My thoughts became a plea to God for help.

I know that God is always with me, and — sure enough — He heard my prayer. A police car, unmistakable even in a foreign country, came into sight at that corner and stopped near the open door of the saloon, a doorway set at an angle. Here was my help!

Quickly I walked to the open window on the driver's side of the patrol car.

"Officer," I said, "can you help me?"

The policeman scarcely turned his head, not wanting to turn from his surveillance of something taking place inside the saloon. In desperation I said, "I'm a woman alone and lost. I have a map with a hotel location marked on it, but I must be going the wrong way. Please help me. . . ."

Reluctantly, and obviously annoyed at being disturbed, he glanced at me. His expression changed slightly. *He must have expected to see one of the neighborhood women!* I thought.

Then he realized that I genuinely needed his help. After a quick glance back into the saloon, he took my map and shook his head.

"Many blocks — that way," he said and pointed at a right angle to the way I had been heading. He handed me the map and immediately turned back to his scrutiny of the saloon.

Grateful to God and to the policeman for even that minimal help, I started walking in the new direction, away from the railroad. *Don't look as if you're lost,* I told myself. *Walk briskly, as if you know where you're going, and don't look around at the other people.*

One block, two blocks, and the character of the neighborhood seemed to be improving. I was passing less shabby commercial buildings and mostly small residences, some with people sitting on the tiny front porches. On and on I went, not looking directly at any of the people. At last the houses took on a look of greater respectability. Feeling more at ease despite my physical weariness, I walked on.

I was nearing a minor business section, completely different from the one behind me, and reasoned that I had surely walked as far in this direction as I should. I turned to my right, saw a small hotel, and went in to speak to the clerk at the desk.

As is often the case at a hotel, the young woman on duty spoke English, and after I'd explained my predicament, she looked at my map and my receipt with the name of the hotel. She didn't recognize the hotel name and shook her head.

"You still have a way to go. Two more blocks that way." She indicated my new direction. "Then go left." She smiled sympathetically. No doubt my tiredness was evident on my face. I thanked her and went as directed.

It was well that I was wearing sturdy, comfortable walking shoes. I continued my unplanned hike, in darkness now but under lighted street

174

lamps. At least I was in a neighborhood that appeared to be respectable. On I went, wondering how much farther I had to go. Surely I must be nearly there! I couldn't see the map well enough to check street names, and I began to feel lost again.

And then I saw a rare sight in an old European city — a modern filling station, on the next corner on the opposite side of the street. Inside its small, brightly lighted office I could see a neatly dressed young man, nothing like the men in the neighborhood from which I had fled. And wonderful, wonderful news awaited me. He even spoke English!

After studying my map, he said, "You are almost there," and pointed to the left. "Just go to that next corner and turn right. It will be in the middle of the block, on your right."

What a relief his words were! That last block and a half was no chore at all. I entered the small lobby of what turned out to be a part-residential, part-transient hotel that had been created by building enclosed bridges to connect several old brick residences with one another.

I was given a key to my room and another to unlock the passageway doors. A problem in finding the room, on an upper floor, was that I had to grope my way through the unlighted passageways. And when I found it, its decor did nothing to lift my spirits. Everything was a dreary brown — walls, draperies, bedspread, carpet. There was a small sink, but the toilet was down the hall, back through one of the unlighted passageways.

Hoping I would not have to get up during the night, I took off my outer clothing and crawled into the bed. What a heartfelt prayer of thanks I said before I closed my eyes! In the morning I would find a hotel near the depot, but for now I had a safe place for the hours of darkness. Yes, God is always with me . . . I had proof positive!

The next morning I returned to the depot by a direct route. That was when I discovered that the main exit was on the street facing the end of Tivoli Gardens, with a lobby area separating it from the big hall. The exit I had seen just beyond the far end of the depot, where I'd expected to find the room-service kiosk, was the one I'd assumed to be the main exit. Thus, by one small oversight we can create great problems for ourselves. Live and learn!

Yes, I should have checked to make sure I knew which way to go. *Oh, those would've, could've, should'ves!* But, on the plus side, perhaps we need those unwanted experiences to help us learn important lessons while we are on this planet.

What did I learn from my long walk that evening, other than that I could keep on going when I thought I'd drop from tiredness?

I can't blame anyone but myself for getting into such a truly dangerous situation, made all the more perilous because I don't know any of the Germanic languages. What would I have done if my purse, containing my passport and money, had been snatched from me? I know that this was one time when fear was justified. The danger was real and I was vulnerable. I was in a much worse situation than when I had locked my keys and purse in my car at Cave-in-Rock.

But if I had panicked outwardly, it would have been worse. I am stronger in my faith in God because of that unpleasant adventure in Copenhagen. Was the timely appearance of the police car coincidence or an answer to my prayer? Was it on the policeman's regular route to stop there? Or did he get a radio message to check that saloon at that time? Did my prayer bring him at that particular moment? I think the answer is in Psalms 4:3: ". . . [T]he Lord will hear when I call unto him."

I truly believe that an instinctive turn to God for help in any crisis — and in between crises too — is vital to my present well-being. It took me many years to learn the truth that help is always available to each of us, but now it is a firm belief.

That lesson, *knowing* that God's help is available if I ask in faith and am receptive to the answers that come, has served me well over and over again since that night on the dark streets of Copenhagen. The help is not limited to times of crisis or trouble. It comes to my aid in small matters too. Sometimes when I've misplaced some item and have looked everywhere, or so it seems,

I ask God where it is. And there it is in the next place I am prompted to look! It's a habit now in matters large and small.

I have other lessons to learn, I'm sure — but not that one. I *know* that the policeman's arrival was not just coincidence.

DOWN MEMORY LANE

The Past Is Part of the Present

After two much more pleasant days in Copenhagen, I used my Eurailpass to take trains and a ferryboat to Oslo, Norway. No problems on my arrival there. That would have really put a damper on things, for my visit to Oslo was on my seventy-sixth birthday!

I had a really lovely, spacious old room there, newly redecorated and with very modern conveniences, even an electric trouser presser, which I didn't need. But the heated towel rack in the bathroom was great! This room, also assigned to me through the tourist service at the train station, turned out to be in a Best Western hotel. It was such a pleasant place that I didn't mind being alone, even on my birthday.

I'd heard about a spectacular train ride from Oslo to Bergen with a side trip down the mountain, via short-line train, to a fiord. The Oslo tourist center helped me arrange that trip, which I took after a fine tour of Oslo. It was really exciting on that tour to see the actual *Kon-Tiki*, the seemingly fragile reed raft on which Thor Heyerdahl made his experimental Pacific Ocean voyage. I also met some friendly Americans on that tour, and I joined them again on the trains to the fiord and to Bergen, which added to the pleasure of a fine day.

We arrived at Bergen, one of my favorite cities, after dark and in rain. I had been to Bergen before with my friend Dot, and we'd had plenty of time for sight-seeing in sunny, cool days. On this current trip, it was still drizzly the next morning, so I headed for the railway depot right after breakfast. One special feature of holding a first-class Eurailpass is that you seldom need a seat reservation and can get on any train as soon as you locate the right passenger car. No waiting in a ticket line! Only once did I have a problem for not having made an advance-seat reservation, when all the first-class coaches from Oslo to Bergen were filled to capacity by a Japanese tour group.

Leaving Bergen, I chose ferry and train service to Amsterdam. I had planned to spend two days there, but upon rethinking my time and route back to Antwerp, I realized I could spend just one day in the city itself before moving on. My days of rail travel were slipping by and it was already too close to Day Fifteen.

On that one day in Amsterdam I had a fine overview of that interesting and unique city from a canal boat. Later, after asking directions from a pleasant and very helpful woman in an information office, I found it easy to use the metropolitan transportation system on my own, seeking some pictures for one of my granddaughters. Everyone seemed fluent in English, and to understand it readily, even when spoken with a Midwestern United States accent! I was sorry to leave so soon, for since childhood I had always wanted to see the beautiful Holland I had imagined while I read *Hans Brinker and the Silver Skates*.

As I rode the train southward from Amsterdam, I had a view of the thriving level countryside the hardworking people of Holland had wrested from the sea and of the gradually rising cultivated land beyond. Then, as the land became more rugged, the train climbed into the low but beautiful Ardennes Mountains in the Grand Duchy of Luxembourg. I disembarked in the old capital city for a pleasant day that included a long walk through a park below the level of most of the city.

The fifteenth and final day that my pass was valid, I was back in Belgium at Namur, only an hour or two from Antwerp, where an afternoon train took me with only seven hours left on my pass. I didn't plan to use those hours. I'd had plenty of train rides!

I took a hotel room because I didn't think the *Otter* was ready for passengers to return. As soon as I reached my hotel room, I opened my carry-on bag of travel-weary clothes and made an unhappy discovery: The slacks to my favorite pantsuit were missing.

And then I remembered. Back at the hotel in Namur, I had noticed they needed mending, as well as laundering, and so I had folded them and placed them on a shelf in the armoire that served as a closet. And, with my head not quite clear because of fighting off a cold, I had left them behind when I packed that morning.

Back to the terminal, fortunately only a block from the hotel. There I took the next train to Brussels and on to Namur, a short distance farther south. My pass was good until midnight, so I had time to go there and back. It was still daylight when I left the train in Namur and hurried to the hotel.

I explained my problem to the clerk at the registration desk and asked if the maid had turned in the slacks.

"No, they're not here," she said. "I'm sorry."

The room had been cleaned but was not occupied, so the clerk let me go up to check it. But when I opened the armoire, there was nothing there. Maybe the slacks were the maid's size. . . .

So the trip back to Namur was all in vain. At least I got my money's worth out of my Eurailpass! I had a light supper in Namur while I awaited a return train to Antwerp. I was back in my room there by eleven, one hour before the pass would expire. But my favorite slacks are with me no more.

It is strange that when we talk to little children

we still tend to call a train a "choo-choo" even though most of today's locomotives are only capable of making a sound more like a moan, now that diesels have taken over the rails. The only "choo-choos" are on short, renovated tourist lines, puffing and chugging their way as in old times.

Enjoying adventures is in my blood, I think, and so is my enjoyment of train travel. The earliest adventure I remember is associated with one of those old smoke-exhaling trains. One summer day when I was about six or seven and brother Jack had just turned eight or nine, we were going to take the train alone from Milwaukee, where we lived, to Madison to stay with one of my mother's sisters for a week or two. Hindsight tells me that this unusual expedition was to get us out of the way while Mother had some surgery.

The adventure began when we took the Thirty-fifth Street trolley by ourselves to get to the railroad depot. "Big brother" Jack was instructed where we were to get off that trolley, at Thirty-fifth and Vliet, and change to another, making sure first that its sign said it would go to the big railway depot in downtown Milwaukee. Dad would leave his office and be watching for our arrival there at five o'clock to see that we got on the train to Madison. Uncle Rudy would be at the depot there to meet us.

Such was the plan, but apparently no one realized that there were *two* different trolley routes that ended at the depot from the Vliet Street track intersections. As fate would have it, we got on the wrong one.

We rode and we rode, but I was enjoying myself tremendously. I had never had the adventure of going on a streetcar without an adult. But when we had been on that streetcar too long for a simple trip downtown, Jack became worried. After all, he was responsible for the two of us! Almost all the other people had left the car, and we still weren't at the depot. We weren't even downtown. Jack sensed that something was wrong and was fighting back tears. There we were in an almost-empty car — and nowhere near the depot.

The conductor realized that all was not well, and he stopped in front of us.

"Where are you two youngsters going?" he asked in a kindly voice.

"We're supposed to go to the depot. Daddy is meeting us there," Jack told him.

"Well, just sit tight," the conductor said and smiled. "This car takes the long way around, but it'll get you there."

And sure enough, it did, after a tour around the city's outskirts. But it was dusk by the time the conductor called out a cheery, "Here we are. The depot, children!" While the motorman waited, the kindly conductor escorted us into the depot, where a woman in a Traveler's Aid uniform hurried over to us. The conductor put us into her care, wished us a good trip, and left. (I have been told that Dad called the carbarn the next day to get the identity of the kind conductor so that he could send him a small reward and a thank-you for his help to us.)

Dad was of course very worried when our intended train to Madison departed and we had not arrived. Finally, he left word at the Traveler's Aid desk to be called immediately if the two of us showed up. He had gone home to see what might have happened and to comfort Mother.

I don't remember being one bit worried. In fact, I was enjoying the whole expedition. Dad, taking the proper trolley, arrived back in the depot in due time and took us to a downtown hotel. Another bit of adventure! I had never been inside a hotel. We had supper, slept a few hours, and were up and dressed while it was still very dark. Downtown Milwaukee streets were almost deserted, but a Thompson's was open. It was a cafeteria with rows of chairs that also served as tables, with a white porcelain surface on the right arm, similar to a student's chair with a wide arm for writing. It was still dark and no other customers were there. I clearly remember a young fellow in his white working clothes doing a cartwheel and handstand on the tiled floor to pass the time — or perhaps to keep himself awake.

Soon after sunrise we were at the depot. Dad took us out to the trainshed where our train stood in readiness, its steam up and hissing as departure time approached. He stayed with us until we were on board and each seated next to a window. And then, with one last big exhaust of steam, the chug-chug-chugging began. I loved to hear the clickety-clack as we sped along, and to see the red barns and white farmhouses of southern Wisconsin's rolling green dairy farmland. We heard the small-town crossing bells grow louder and higher pitched as we approached. They faded to silence as we went on our way, leaving a trail of dark smoke we could see when we rounded curves.

Uncle Rudy met us at the depot in Madison, ending the marvelous adventure that lingers in memory. I'm sure the chief cause of our excitement was the feeling of independence, of freedom from adult supervision. For the two of us to be traveling alone was a major adventure!

Years later, returning home for Christmas vacation from college at Stevens Point, Wisconsin, I took a train to the huge Union Station in Chicago. Part of a return trip to Stevens Point after a heavy snowstorm is vivid in memory. High banks of snow slowed the puffing locomotive, but we young folks didn't mind a bit. I clearly remember that we were in a car that was an antique even then. It had no electric power, and when darkness came, a trainman had to place a step stool under each of the hanging light fixtures over the aisle and hand-light them.

In 1933, a new kind of train was ready to take the place of the old steam-powered ones. I saw it with a group of friends at the Century of Progress Exposition, celebrating Chicago's centennial year. A major exhibit was devoted to the first diesel passenger train. Its silvery exterior was so different from the old trains that it was described as "stream-lined," a new term at that time. We walked through that unique train, and the next year it went into service, the prototype for the new trains in years to come. Its horn, somehow, lacks the charm of the old steam train's lonesome call on the prairies of the Midwest.

A few years ago, when I was going for a Christmas visit to my daughter Mary in California, I had no wish to put up with airport hassle at the holiday season, so I opted for Amtrak. I was tired from a busy schedule when I started on the trip, and I loved the three leisurely days on the train. I had a roomette, with daytime seating that became a bed at night and with sliding doors to close it off from the aisle. I'll probably do that again on some future visits to the West Coast. It's a relaxing way to travel, with or without a companion.

Many short-line steam-engine trains are now giving tourists the feel of the old choo-choos. It's an adventure to ride them and learn how previous generations traveled, without air-conditioning and with flying cinders when windows or doors were opened. I've had that nostalgic adventure recently. Just last year I rode two of those tourist-attraction antique trains. My friend Dot was with me on one of them, a spectacular mountain-pass ride from Chama, New Mexico, to Antonito, Colorado.

Dot and I also chose to go by train instead of tour bus in Switzerland from Davos to glamorous Saint Moritz. I think of that breathtaking ride through the Alps every time I don my sweat shirt with the Saint Moritz emblem to go out and do my plebeian yard work on a cool autumn day. Reliving my Swiss adventure takes away the tedium of hard work.

Another really fun train adventure was with my daughter Mary in the British Isles, after a Saga cruise on the Danube River. We had a week's prepaid hotel lodging in London and a pair of BritRail passes. Mary didn't want the usual tourist things — she wanted adventure. We rode the trains every day, seeking castles, and we found them, some in ruins and others still housing British dukes. We learned to use the underground, their subway, like old-timers, riding several different branches. London doesn't use a central terminal, and its many railroads connect with the underground at various stations. On most days we left the city in the morning and returned at night.

To start our week, we took the fast new train to Edinburgh to visit the famed fortress castle on the mountain. We spent a night at a lovely old hotel there before returning to London. Another day we took the train to Cardiff in Wales, to tour one of the more elegant castles. Going from Cardiff to Caerphilly, via a side line of the rail system, was a contrast in both trains and castles. Caerphilly Castle was partially in ruins, complete with a leaning tower and a moat still with water instead of the grass to which most old castle or fortress moats have been converted.

The passenger cars on that little side-line railroad were leftovers from another day. The one we were in was the kind we used to see in the old movies. It had individual exit doors from each passenger compartment, doors you open yourself. In trying to get the door open, we almost didn't make it out of the car when we reached our station at Caerphilly a bit sooner than we expected!

I hope our own country develops more and more train travel for people not in too much of a hurry. You see the land up close, mountains and plains alike, and often go through the old part of cities and towns, where signal bells clang and gates hold back the automobiles. And we passengers can simply relax and let our thoughts flow as we gaze at the passing scenery.

Airplanes get us there when time is important, but with their ever-increasing size and speed, they're like the rest of today's world — too crowded and in too much of a hurry. We hurry to get into another line, only to stand and wait, fuming at delay. The rails offer the leisurely way to go, and it's a lot more fun than going by air!

Many of my favorite adventures have taken me away from the big cities. Both at home and abroad, the cities have become so much alike in these days of franchised businesses. The pace is faster and faster. The day for most people is all too often too hurried and harried to allow time for relaxation of body and receptivity of mind. We can't turn back the clock to a less frenetic era, but now and then we can take a relaxing time out and perhaps glimpse some of the marvels of pre-neon-sign days.

Have you ever been in an unsettled area without street-lights or even electricity and then looked up at the amazing firmament? Now, that's a very special kind of adventure! To my family and to me, city dwellers all, the night sky was a revelation when we had an opportunity to really see it, away from city lights.

In the 1940s my parents moved to an Ozark house not far from my present one, when this was still a rural location and the neighboring farm-houses seldom had yard lights. On cloudy nights, the darkness outdoors was deep, but on clear nights, what celestial glories brightened the way!

When my family and I came to visit my parents back then, we would sit outdoors in lawn chairs on clear summer nights and do nothing but gaze at the stars, taking turns with the binoculars. The Milky Way was an awesome wonder. I have never forgotten those hours of stargazing in the Ozarks. The Milky Way was a pathway to "the peace that passes all understanding."

Even after I came here to live in 1955, the night sky was magnificent. I'd watch each autumn evening for the appearance in the east of the great constellation Orion, the hunter in the sky. To the north the Great Dipper pointed the way clearly to the North Star. But in recent years yard lights and streetlights have multiplied, and now only the brightest of the planets and stars can be seen. I miss those old times. . . .

The beautiful old hymn "How Great Thou Art" may well have been inspired by the overwhelming beauty of the night sky, which we can still see in the rare areas where artificial light hasn't robbed us of its full glory:

> O Lord, my God, when I in awesome
> wonder
> Consider all the worlds thy hands have
> made:
> I see the stars, I hear the rolling
> thunder,
> Thy pow'r throughout the universe
> displayed.

We live in a time of great progress, and who would want to turn back the clock to the days before the electric light and all the other conveniences of electricity? Still, I miss seeing the old night sky.

Yet, like our memories of past adventures and happy times, the stars are as close to us as our imagination. The Milky Way, the Big Dipper, and Orion are still there. We don't have to go out of doors to see them. All we have to do is close our eyes and enjoy the blessing of memory.

"God's in his heaven — / All's right with the world!" wrote the poet Robert Browning. And it is true. The stars are still there, and God's universe is still displayed. They are never dimmed by man-made lights when we see them with our heart.

LASTING TREASURES

Our Own Private Miracles

Some things we see or hear are so striking that we say, "I'll never forget that!" Three years have passed since a certain night while I was a passenger on the cargo liner *Howell Lykes*, when I saw a sight that was truly unforgettable. I need only close my eyes and there it is again — spectacular, almost frightening, awesome and yet beautiful.

Earlier that Sunday, the *Howell Lykes* was in the harbor at Naples, Italy, with Mount Vesuvius in sight but dimmed by rain showers. Cargo loading was finally completed in midafternoon, and we left for a return visit to Livorno, our final docking in the Mediterranean. We were due to reach port by morning. After two days there, with time to visit Pisa and even Florence, it would be a long way to the next port — New York City.

In the late afternoon we were passing Rome, hidden though it was by distance and low-lying clouds. I was out on the deck, and as I leaned against a varnished mahogany deck rail on this majestic old lady of a ship, I conjured up the places she had been in her glory years. When I first became a freighter addict, she was the *President Van Buren*, one of the President Line's finer ships, and she cruised the Pacific Ocean to the South Seas. I applied for passage on a "grab bag voyage," so-named because the foreign ports were so varied they were not specified in advance. I was waitlisted for more than two years. Then one day a call came that a single cabin was available. But the sailing was at a poor time for me, and, also, in those years of inflation and rising oil prices, the cost of passage had doubled since I applied. I deeply regretted — and still do — losing that opportunity to go to the exotic South Sea Islands, and certainly this old dowager ship would never tell me what I had missed.

On that gray, drippy day in the Mediterranean, as I mused and gazed down into the foamy water, I was mentally touring those South Sea Islands. I came back to the present when someone came by. Then, looking up, I saw there were patches of blue in the leaden sky. Perhaps fair weather was coming.

Later, as darkness approached, we were quite close to the Italian coast and could occasionally see the low line of hills and mountains ashore. The air was warm and moist. An occasional rumble of thunder indicated that clearing was not yet complete. About eight o'clock, curious about the progress of the clearing skies, I had an urge to go out onto the deck again before settling down for the night in my luxurious bedroom. As I went out onto the open deck, the coastal hills to the east were partially blocked from view by low-lying clouds.

"*Oh!* Superb!" No one else was out there, but I had to say it aloud as a spectacular show began. A little to the left of the Italian shoreline, above the bank of clouds, hung the newly risen, glorious October moon, a great shining ball only slightly past full. On the sea, heading directly toward me as I stood at the deck rail, it sent a broad, silvery path of shimmering light across the water.

I watched transfixed. The huge moon hovered there like a lighted balloon, illuminating that water pathway and the dimly seen shoreline of low hills. Above the moon, spread out in that vast up-side-down bowl of sky, was a great, wide, slanting band of white buttermilk clouds.

But on the horizon farther to my left, the moon-light also touched upon rolling thunderclouds. Suddenly, as I stood transfixed, there came a great zigzag of lightning — brilliant, electrifying — slashing into that mass of dark cloud. And then came an overwhelming crescendo of thunder.

As the crashing rolls of thunder continued, the sky lighted again and again, flashes overlapping like big fireworks displays. The constant flashing not only revealed the boiling black clouds but also amplified the moonlight on the dappled white sash of buttermilk sky, stretching from the edge of the storm area to the Italian shore, and toward me until I lost sight of it above the ship.

The storm raged violently, too far away for the rain to reach our ship. Simultaneously, sublimely, as if all was calm, the "moon river" on the sea's surface flowed on undisturbed, from its brilliant source to the lacy foam alongside the quietly gliding ship.

Of course I went to my cabin to get my camera on the chance that its completely automated works might catch that marvelous waterway vista. Weeks later, when my film was developed, all that showed was the moon and its watery path. The marvel of the full scene was lost. This was one time I wished that I had packed my heavier camera, the one with which I can take time exposures. The print I have can only act as a spur to memory of the amazing spectacle, just a confirmation that I witnessed a gorgeous, active scene on that moon-and-storm-lit October night on the Mediterranean Sea. But my mind's eye sees the real scene vividly as I write, years later. . . .

No ad from a travel agency could have forecast that vista. It was one of those blessings that are poured into the lap of a fortunate traveler. And what an awesome blessing it was!

No one was about as I stood there, watching nature's sound and light show. I was filled with the wonder of it all. God's creation surpasses anything that we humans, His instruments of expression on earth, can fashion. To my mind, even the most complex of computerized and electronic inventions do not rival nature's prime-time shows.

To me, those minutes of standing out there, alone on that deck, not seeing another human being, are a special gift from God, a time when I was a privileged witness to His miraculous wonders.

Life itself is a miracle, and I am among the most fortunate of the living. But each of us, in that marvelous storehouse we carry with us constantly, can conjure up our own memories that do not fade. Our "unforgettable" can be a special time, perhaps a rainbow in the east as a rain shower ends and the low western sun does its magic. It may be a panorama from a high window in the city, when the early-morning light veils the roofs that seem so mundane a few hours later, or lilac bushes sparkling in the morning sun after a freezing rain. These are treasures in our mental storehouse to bring us pleasure for so long as we shall continue in this life.

How grateful we all should be, just for being alive to experience these marvels, these special gifts that come to us, almost always unexpectedly. I remember a great double rainbow out on the western plains, the welcome rumble of thunder and the pelt of raindrops on dry, sunbaked ground, the smoothness of a baby's skin, the smell of freshly baked bread. We each have our own memories that make life more meaningful to body, mind, and spirit. They are treasures, each and every one, and reliving them is a way to bring joy to ourselves over and over again.

"Take time to smell the roses," we hear. We should take time, also, to gaze at our world around us, close to home or far away. Sooner or later, we will have another mental picture in our personal storehouse of the unforgettable.

"DON'T WORRY — BE HAPPY!"

Who Needs More Wrinkles?

It is late on a September afternoon in 1990, and I am walking alongside a middle-aged Egyptian man between rows of cargo containers stacked on a dock in Alexandria, Egypt. The Egyptian, dark and portly, well dressed in a white suit, Panama hat, and shiny black shoes, reminds me of the villain in the old black-and-white movies. I had never seen him until an hour ago, and I am entrusting my security — my very life, some would say — to him. It is not a reassuring thought.

I look back at the superstructure of the *Howell Lykes* and see the windows of the lovely suite I call home while on this voyage. A strange set of circumstances has resulted in my being the only remaining woman passenger of the five who sailed from New York. The only male passenger who might have joined me on a tour has been to Egypt repeatedly. I have never been here before and have been looking forward to a trip to Cairo while the ship is docked at nearby Alexandria. But now, alone with this intimidating Egyptian gentleman, I'm tempted to hurry back to safety aboard ship even though it would mean foregoing my sight-seeing.

I am about to say, "I've changed my mind."

But the Egyptian, introduced to me as Mr. Mohamed, speaks first. "The minibus is air-conditioned," he informs me, and nods toward a parking lot just beyond the dock gates. I continue to walk alongside him in silence.

A much younger Egyptian man stands waiting outside the minibus as we approach. He grins widely, showing very white teeth. He also wears white, but not a suit, just an open-necked shirt and slacks.

"My son Mohamed," my escort says. I know from his business card that he is Mohamed, Sr., owner of a travel agency in Alexandria. He speaks to his son in Egyptian while I stand waiting. I am sure he is telling Junior the disappointing news that I am the only tourist on the big freighter who is available for the Cairo trip. Then they turn to me and indicate I should get into the minibus. A third Egyptian man sits at the steering wheel.

"Air-conditioned," Junior says with pride in his voice. He smiles at me as he waves his hand to indicate the interior. This seems to him to be a matter of exceptional merit, and perhaps it is unusual, but I'm not impressed with that information. I have just realized that I am to be the only woman and foreigner in the minibus.

The drumbeat to which I dance my dance of

life slows at this moment, and drops to a dirgelike tempo, in line with the sinking feeling I am experiencing. What have I gotten myself into?

But it's too late to back out without an excuse. I climb in and take a seat behind the driver, who neither looks at me nor speaks. Both Mohameds get into the bus, and Mohamed, Sr., turns to look at me.

"Don't worry — be happy!" he says, and I realize that my concern must be reflected on my face. I force a weak smile.

We drive into an old part of the city where laundry is strung on lines from shallow second-floor balconies to pulleys attached to second-floor window frames on the opposite side of the narrow street. We stop, double-parked, in heavy traffic, to a cacophony of horn beeps. Mohamed, Sr., gets out. I am told to follow him into a building.

I find I am in Mohamed's travel-agency office, where I am requested to pay for my projected excursion. It will be nearly two A.M. when we return to Alexandria, so I must pay now. I haggle a bit, but Mohamed, Sr., will drop only three dollars from his price. We leave him in his office, and then I am alone in the minibus with Mohamed, Jr., and the driver, who, I soon discover, speaks no English at all.

Junior looks back at me, grins again, and in his heavily accented voice, echoes his father in a hearty, "Don't worry — be happy!" before he turns away.

I take a deep breath, and then pray silently as we begin the 135-mile drive to Cairo, to the almost continuous beeping of the horn. I, an elderly American woman, am alone and in the care of two strangers speaking their unintelligible language in the front of the minibus. *Don't worry — be happy!* echoes in my mind. I didn't know at the time that this was the name of a song then popular in the United States and no doubt heard on the radio in Egypt.

After all, I reflect, I have chosen to go on this night excursion rather than miss seeing the famed Great Pyramids and the Sphinx, because the hours before my ship sails are limited. I have had to discard a planned overnight stay in a Cairo hotel. My intent had been to share a cab through the green delta area down to Cairo with a young American passenger who works to aid Egyptian farmers. He would not be returning to the ship, but he had recommended a hotel for me in Cairo. This plan would have permitted me to attend the sound-and-light show at the Sphinx and Great Pyramids in the evening and have a morning sight-seeing tour before taking a bus back to Alexandria.

But soon after we docked at Alexandria, this great plan had collapsed. The young man's reentry permit had to go through unexpected red tape before he could leave the ship, but the real change of schedule was because, when we docked, a crew to handle the cargo was ready to start work immediately instead of in the morning, as the captain had expected. The next day's projected late-afternoon departure from Alexandria had been moved back to eight in the morning.

There would be no chance for the planned overnight trip down to Cairo, and becoming the only passenger on this night excursion was my only chance to see all those wonders of ancient Egypt.

I try to reassure myself with the reminder that Mohamed, Sr., was the only travel agent allowed to board the ship with the captain's approval, and so he must be reliable. Before making my decision, I had taken a few minutes in my cabin to listen to my inner voice, the spirit that had guided me through many another strange adventure, and was told to go ahead.

Don't worry — be happy! Good advice, indeed, for anyone. I begin to relax as the minibus turns onto a wide boulevard along a bay. Worry accomplishes nothing except to disturb the worrier's physical chemistry, I reflect. Chances are I'll get back to the ship safely.

My dance of life drumbeat gradually resumes a near-normal tempo, only slowing when I permit those "what if" thoughts to recur. I am still somewhat uneasy about my personal safety, but I try to reassure myself that these two men have no sinister intentions toward me. This could be a great adventure, I decide as we leave the city and start south on a horn-beeping trip on the four-lane highway through the desert to Cairo — and a night I've never forgotten.

After a few minutes, thinking that Mohamed

is the family surname, I ask my guide to tell me his first name.

"Mohamed," he answers. Then he adds, "You can call me Jimmy."

Jimmy — that's a bit more comfortable for me. Jimmy knows just enough English to communicate in rudimentary fashion, heavily accented. He gestures toward the passing scenery, or lack of it, as he turns to speak to me.

"Dessertroat," he says.

I nod and finally figure out he means the obvious — desert road. The bleak landscape helps in my interpretation. He turns back to the driver and they converse in Egyptian. With conversation impossible for me, I sit in silence, clutching the seat arm as we speed along on this major highway.

But I am the only silent one. The two men talk steadily in their own language, to the accompaniment of the horn's nearly continuous beep as the driver makes his way around every vehicle on our side of the four-lane divided highway. Or rather, in the middle of our half of the four-lane highway, for that seems to be where all the drivers choose to stay. I'm sure the minibus's engine would die if not for the stimulation of the beeping. I become aware of another sound, a high-pitched continuous bell signal, which I finally decide comes on when the driver's foot gets a bit heavy on the accelerator. The bell signal sounds most of the time.

We pull in at a roadside gas station with the familiar name Mobil. Both men get out, and while the tank is being filled, Jimmy disappears into the convenience store. He has small packages when he gets back into the van.

He turns to me and says, "For you," and hands me a package of Chiclets, with the name in English on one side and in Arabic on the other. Later we stop again, and this time, having noted that I had been bothered by a tension-produced cough, he brings out Hall's cough lozenges, also labeled on one side in English and in Arabic on the other.

We get underway again, and again I am admonished with a lighthearted grin that shows strong white teeth, "Don't worry — be happy!" I try to comply as I unwrap a lozenge.

On that late-September day, darkness came long before we entered the city of Cairo. Soon we crossed the Nile again into Giza, which is the location of the pyramids and the Sphinx. And what a time we had there!

It was a busy evening in Giza. Most of the town's families must have been out and about. Traffic was bumper to bumper, and the walks were crowded with people plus a few donkeys with panniers on their sides, usually loaded with produce. Pedestrians made their way with some difficulty, often stepping into the street because of the many merchants who had spread their wares on the sidewalks.

Except for a few of the younger men and women, the people in Giza were wearing the traditional Arab dress, in contrast to the predom-

204

inantly Western garb on Cairo streets. Even though the night was warm, the women were in their black chadors. On the other hand, the men wore the more comfortable lightweight costume on this summer evening, similar to an ankle-length nightshirt, instead of the robelike djellaba. The children wore similar long garments, but often of a printed fabric. All wore sandals, usually of plastic rather than leather.

As we turned into a narrow and crowded street, I heard above all the street noise an amplified voice intoning a religious reading.

"Koran," Jimmy informed me. Apparently this was a Muslim holiday weekend of some kind.

The block into which we turned, heading west, would have been none too wide for two lanes of traffic going in opposite directions under normal conditions. But on this night, the two lines of traffic were attempting to move in both directions on only half of the street width for the length of that block. The half to our left had been torn up into a yawning ditch that looked deep enough to hold a car. There were no safety barricades, only two-by-six planks laid along the edge of the gaping excavation. Here and there, more planks of random lengths were standing at odd angles vertical to the chasm.

The sensible thing would have been to make this block a one-way street, alternating directions with traffic controllers, such as we often encounter on our highways in safety-conscious America. Not so in Giza! It was the worst traffic mess I have ever seen, surpassing even the streets in Rome at the noon hour. No one controlled the bumper-to-bumper streams of cars, and nobody held back for even a few seconds to let a blockage get opened.

Occasionally, when the oncoming eastbound vehicle was a bit wider than the usual small cars, our westbound van rode with its right wheels on the sidewalk. And the sidewalk itself was unlike those we have in our well-maintained towns. It dropped down intermittently to a lower level of pavement, or rose from street to walk. For much of the distance there seemed to be no pavement, just gravelly sand from the desert.

Eventually, we reached the end of that block and a bit more travel room. The outdoor theater was two or three blocks farther. The light-and-sound performance is often repeated each evening in three different languages to accommodate tourists. Our purpose in this difficult approach was to get to the theater so that Jimmy could learn the time of the English version, which turned out to be nine-thirty. We had two hours to spare. Within minutes we were back in that infamous block, heading eastward on the side adjacent to the big hole in the street.

The two-by-sixes that edged the excavation were laid randomly. We reached a point at which the van could not get moving again because it needed to get the right-side wheels onto the next plank. And there we sat amidst beeping horns. Frustrated, our driver got out and walked back along the line of cars behind us. Somehow he got them all to back up about half a car length. With this leeway, he backed up the van and then urged it forward and onto the planks. And we didn't fall into the ditch!

On another street, he parked the van and Jimmy took me on the requisite tour of places to spend my money. I wasn't very agreeable to the idea, since my funds were dwindling rapidly. I did go willingly into the papyrus shop, where I watched a brief demonstration of the making of this predecessor to paper, from the reed stalk to the finished product. Very fine, hand-colored drawings on papyrus were available, and I purchased three. They were to be individualized with a cartouche of the name of each future recipient written in hieroglyphics, and I was to pick them up after the show.

Back in modern Cairo, we made our way to the fine hotel where dinner was to be served to me, part of the package. Jimmy escorted me to the restaurant. I was free to order anything from the menu, but by this time there was only a half hour before we had to make our way back to the Giza theater. I settled for a needed rest-room visit and a sandwich and a soft drink when I was back at the table.

The return to the theater through the blocked street was even slower than the previous maneuvering of the narrow confines. Halfway down the block we came to a complete standstill, and Jimmy got out of the van.

"Come, we walk," he said, and opened the side door for me.

So then I had another wild experience. He grasped my left hand and we half galloped, half walked our way along, one foot on the walk and one in the street most of the time. We squeezed around a donkey and sidewalk sales displays, and finally we reached the grounds of the theater.

Jimmy bought my ticket and handed it to me. "One hour. I watch for you," he said, and left.

I went in and found a good seat facing the Sphinx. The Great Pyramid was off a little to the right behind it, and two lesser pyramids were somewhat farther away and a little to the left. While spotlights illumined the pyramid or the Sphinx, the sound system brought music and an interesting recording about its history.

At the end of the performance, I came out amidst the crowd of Americans and other English-speaking people and looked for Jimmy. I saw him some thirty feet away, watching for me. He waved happily and called out in a loud voice, "Here I am, *darling!*"

Can you imagine the looks that came my way? I covered up my embarrassment by holding my camera to my face as I said, "I'll take your picture!"

Our return was not entirely without incident. For example, we drove right across the median when Jimmy wanted to stop at a lighted store on the other side. This time he brought out a soft drink for me. Let it be said that I made it safely back to the ship just before two in the morning.

With men loitering about, I didn't want to walk alone through the container dock to the ship at that hour, and I was glad and relieved when Jimmy offered to escort me when we had to leave the van outside the gate.

Among my souvenirs is one of the papyrus drawings, now framed, and my photograph of Jimmy, with his "don't worry — be happy!" smile.

Some people would say I was taking a terrible chance in agreeing to go on this nighttime expedition. An American woman alone in a strange land where the culture was so different from my own, I had entrusted myself to the care of two Egyptians for seven hours and 270 miles of travel. I agree — I *was* taking a chance. And for a while, I was quite worried. A natural reaction, I'm sure.

But what difference would it have made if I had spent the whole seven hours thinking thoughts of terrible possibilities? It certainly wouldn't have changed the actual events, and I'd have missed the positive enjoyment that was part of the adventure. The difference would have been in hurting only myself. Worry, like all negative emotions and thoughts, can damage the human body through destructive chemical reactions, a fact that physicians are recognizing.

Don't worry — be happy! Good advice! Once we have made a decision and the time has passed for a change of plans, worrying is an exercise in wrinkle growing. And who wants more wrinkles? By the time I was run-walking in Giza with Jimmy, I had ceased all worry, and I did not worry at all about the long drive back to the ship in the depth of night on an almost deserted desert road.

Is it significant that, after having a Mohamed as my guide in Egypt, when I reached Haifa, Israel, my tour guide turned out to be "Holy Joe"? No kidding. I have his card. And he was an excellent guide for my solo trip to the land where Jesus walked.

BY THE SEA OF GALILEE

Getting in Touch with God

The *Howell Lykes* seemed impatient to get underway from Alexandria, or was it just the feeling of the passengers leaning over the deck rail on that fine sunshiny day in late September? But she sat there for hours after the posted eight A.M. sailing time. No one can do much to expedite an embarkation when very impressive conferences are being held on the dock and in the captain's quarters!

Jim, the young man assigned to upgrade farming practices on the rich delta lands, would be remaining in Egypt. By now we had said our farewells to him, and he was down on the dock with all the boxes and bundles he'd brought from America, awaiting the driver who would take him down the Delta Road, a highway far more attractive, Jim had said, than the Desert Road. The road was one of the benefits from tragic days of World War II, when it had been built under the direction of the German Field Marshal Erwin Rommel, the "Desert Fox."

211

Jim was hemmed in by a circle of Egyptian men, all seemingly very vociferous. Finally a small truck arrived alongside the ship, and Jim and his goods were soon on their way to the delta. Even then we didn't get going. More Egyptian officialdom had to finish their examinations on board, to make sure that our captain was not overlooking any minutia of the regulations.

But finally the delays ended. The last Egyptian left the ship and the gangway was raised to its resting place alongside the bulwarks of the deck where the shipping containers were stacked. At last we were underway to the eastern extreme of the Mediterranean Sea, to the port of Haifa in Israel.

This time there was no need for a hurried land tour. We had dropped anchor in the harbor around four A.M. on Saturday, where we remained about twenty-four hours, plenty of time to rest after my Egyptian adventure. We soon realized that docking was delayed because this was Israel's sabbath.

By breakfasttime, the mists were lifting from the turquoise-blue water and Haifa was clearly visible from the decks. It looked like a pleasant city, ascending from the sea in three very apparent tiers. I soon learned from the radio officer, who was a geography professor on sabbatical, that this slope was the seaward side of Mount Carmel, rising from the Bay of Acre, where our ship would dock.

"What you see most clearly from here at dock

level," he pointed out, "is the least-attractive part of the city. It's the commercial and manufacturing sector, the area the sailors head for when they have leave. Look above it to the next terrace. Right over there." He pointed to the heart of that sector as he added, "Do you see that glint of gold?"

The glint of gold was from the dome of a famed Baha'i temple, he explained. The middle level where it was located was also Haifa's main residential and shopping center. On this sunny day the dome stood out plainly. The temple was a well-known landmark.

Later, when I toured the city, I had the opportunity to see the gold-domed temple at close view. It stood in the Temple Garden, several acres of twisted old olive trees among other plantings. As I walked through the Temple Garden, I thought that the biblical Garden of Gethsemane near Jerusalem was probably similar, for "gethsemane" means "oil press."

Atop Mount Carmel, crowning the city, was an area of large white hotels, palatial new residences, the university, and other cultural institutions. There were also parkways with marvelous views of the harbor and surrounding countryside below.

All this and a great deal more I saw with tour guide "Holy Joe," a balding man of about forty. He was a quiet-mannered gentleman who came aboard the *Howell Lykes* early on Sunday morning after we had docked. Again, business for tour guides was confined to whatever I chose, as the other remaining passenger, a retired Jewish professor of languages, had toured Israel many times on other visits.

Holy Joe handed me his business card and introduced himself. I smiled at the nickname printed on the card under his real name. The "Joe" was obvious, for his given name was Joseph.

"Why are you called 'Holy Joe'?" I asked.

He smiled. "My surname, in Hebrew, means 'pious' — 'holy' sounds better," he explained. I agreed that it was a catchy term for his tour-guide business, considering that most of his expeditions would be on what many consider to be holy ground.

My first impression of Holy Joe was very favorable. I was not in the least worried about placing myself in his care for the day. He had two major expeditions to offer. One was down to Jerusalem, where most of his clients went. The other was to the area north of Jerusalem, featuring Nazareth and the Sea of Galilee, the lands where Jesus had walked and preached with his disciples during those three years of his ministry. I felt that Jerusalem was probably affected by American culture and tourism, like all the other major cities, and would not be nearly as spiritually helpful to me as a trip to the Sea of Galilee area. Very soon we had agreed upon a price and were on the way in his car.

My preconceived impression of the Israeli countryside was of a desert area with occasional groves of palm and fig trees. Well, yes, the fig trees were there, and so were the palms, but the land was rolling, and even mountainous to about the same extent as my home area, the Ozarks. And it was lushly green for the most part.

My idea of the appearance of the site of Jesus' first miracle, turning water to wine, was also way off. I had thought it would be a disappointment, with no traces left of the Cana of Jesus' time. But when we reached Cana, I had only to mentally whisk away a few modern structures, one of them the souvenir building and its advertising sign. But even the sign was so unique that I took a picture of it. It was a board about twenty inches high and perhaps eight feet long attached near the top of an ancient rock wall. The words SOUVENIRS OF CANA IN GALILEE led up to a small painting of Jesus performing the miracle. Next to the painting, the signboard artist switched abruptly into modern times and he began promoting the local vineyard product. In big, bold letters were the words CANA WINES and beside them a large, modern wine bottle was painted.

But this was almost the only sign of modernity I saw in Cana. Above the sign, atop the ancient stone wall, was a row of big clay urns that could well have been old. I could picture quite easily how the settlement of Cana might have appeared two thousand years ago. The narrow, winding, stone main street was no more than eight feet in breadth and not likely to be widened because it was confined between more of the ancient stone

walls. Cana is only about five miles north of Nazareth, so we were actually in Jesus' home area.
It was highly likely that Nazarenes would come
to Cana for a special wedding feast, and it wasn't
difficult to transpose myself mentally to the first
century A.D.

Right across the narrow road behind the souvenir shop, the gates to a churchyard were open.
My visit was on a Sunday, and neatly dressed
people were gathering there for mass. I could
see an open courtyard and beyond it the church
facade. The hand-cut stone structure looked old
enough to have been built in early Christian days.
Perhaps it had replaced a temple that was there
when Jesus and his mother, Mary, attended the
famed Cana wedding feast. I've always thought
it interesting that Jesus' mother urged Jesus on
to produce more wine for the wedding guests.
How proud and yet mystified she must have been
when her son performed that miracle, his first
in public!

It didn't bother me that modern-day promoters
had taken a liberty, no doubt with tourists in
mind, and posted a sign on the church entrance
— *The Wedding Church*. I could ignore the anach-
ronism that a Christian church had been there
when Jesus performed his miracle. Looking up
that old street I could easily feel that, yes, this
was holy ground.

Cana set the mood for the entire expedition.
I found myself easily transported nearly two thousand years into the past. The sensation deepened

when we stopped at a garden and church that memorialized the feeding of the multitudes, and that sense of spiritual kinship increased as the day went on. Before long, we were in the highlands, looking down at the sparkling waters of the Sea of Galilee.

"See that long ridge on the west bank?" Joe pointed as he spoke. "That's the Golan Heights you've probably read so much about in the newspapers."

The heights, veiled in purple mist, reached the length of the sea. On the near shore, below the ridge on which we stood, was a modern city with white buildings that appeared to be hotels.

"Tiberias," Joe said.

The land from the place where we stood near the road drops quite abruptly to a gentle slope and beach. Tiberias doesn't lend itself to a feeling of antiquity, for it has become a modern resort center, and I was glad we didn't go down into the town until we were about to leave the Sea of Galilee area. Instead, we turned to follow the blacktop road to the north, following the shoreline and gradually descending nearer to the level of the Sea of Galilee, to our right. We were on the way to Capernaum and close to the site of the Sermon on the Mount, which Jesus, in a high place both spiritually and physically, delivered to his disciples on the lower slopes.

Along the way, there was little to interfere with my mental transference to biblical times. When Holy Joe stopped the car for me to explore, as he obligingly did whenever I asked, I walked down the slope and alongside the sea where the disciples cast their nets.

I had not realized that the Sea of Galilee, known in Israel as "Yam [Lake] Kinneret," is about 680 feet below sea level. When I got back into the car, Holy Joe explained to me the modern technicalities of water flow and removal of salt water from a spring in the sea floor. This information I have forgotten for the most part, but ever in my mind will be the remains of ancient Capernaum. Abandoned a millennium ago, the site had been home to only a few Arab families until archaeological restoration began in 1968. I left Joe and the car by the gate and went wandering about at my leisure, with no order to "be back in the bus in thirty minutes," as I would have heard had I been part of a large tour group.

In semirestored Capernaum, the present roofless "white temple" in which one can walk about is above the "black temple" (named for the structural rock) where Jesus taught many times. One can still feel his presence there and in the other ruins. Peter's house, where Jesus stayed, was fenced off because of reconstructive work in progress, but the exterior gave me plenty to contemplate. Walking beyond the excavated town to land sloping down to the shore of the sea, I was much aware that I was walking where Jesus walked, and I could almost see his disciples' fishing boats along the shore below.

What a fine day I had with Holy Joe! We

lunched in an open pavilion along the River Jordan. Afterward, down on the riverbank, I watched as a Greek Orthodox priest baptized babies in the river's waters. Then it was time to head westward for the return to Haifa. Modern times had taken over in Nazareth, our major stop. Nothing there or in the rest of the tour, which included a kibbutz, was as moving as the morning's scenes. I send my thanks to Holy Joe for guiding me so graciously that Sunday, September 30, 1990, and for the gift of making it possible for me to walk at leisure where Jesus walked in Capernaum and along the shores of the Sea of Galilee.

Sometimes it takes us the greater part of our lives to feel the need to open ourselves to spirituality. Through the years when I was raising my family, working as a teacher, and even later as a writer, I had had no realization of my need to find a balance in living that included the spiritual.

My physical self, plus my mind and accomplishments in work, formed my concept of the total *ME*. I had much to learn. One significant fact I was unaware of was how much our thought processes influence our bodily health. Looking back on the agony of a blocked gallbladder when I was forty-nine, I now see a definite relationship between the bitterness that was building in my mind at that time, when I felt my marriage was an empty charade, and the physical bitterness and blockage in my gallbladder. I passed the fifty-year mark freed of the gallbladder, but still in pain from other unsolved problems. The beat of my dance of life had slowed alarmingly.

The relationship of mind activity to bodily health becomes obvious if we really give thought to it. Who has not felt the rush of adrenaline brought on, not by an actual physical trauma such as an automobile accident, but by the sudden, frightening *thought* that we might be about to experience something awful? We can't doubt that the body's chemistry is closely linked to mind activity, and that chemical/neurological imbalance can create havoc with bodily health and sometimes with mental health. There are many studies that demonstrate various aspects of this truth.

I have known the fundamentals of body nourishment since the long-ago days of my mother's insistence that I eat my vegetables and drink my milk — and not one bite of dessert until I'd eaten all that was on my dinner plate! Mind nourishment also needs a balanced diet, and I had to get past the yen for more and more of the trivia I had fed my mind in my youth. Now I have learned to keep my mind active and fed with new interests and ideas, research, and exploration of new places, whether actually visited or visualized through reading and other media.

I had danced alone for a number of years before I realized that I had a deep need for spiritual nourishment. I remember saying aloud one evening when I felt discouraged and overwhelmed by problems, "God, I've made a mess of things!

220

Please help me!" Without realizing it, I was taking the first step of many self-improvement programs. I had at last recognized that there is a Power greater than myself, and I was surrendering to that Power.

As He always does, God heard my cry and answered it. For I am sure it was not just by chance that I was soon led to a study group where I discovered what was for me a wonderful new concept of God. This was not the God of my childhood, who was to be feared as the great avenger somewhere "up there." God, I learned, is all good, an omnipresent help to everyone who sincerely "asks, seeks and knocks" for the door to be opened, as we are encouraged to do in Luke 11:9. He speaks to us through an inner voice, and He is always there, ready and willing to lead us along the right path to the good available to each of us — if we will only listen.

At last I had found my personal God, always present, always available. I had never before understood how God could care about me, one person among the earth's billions! Through my study group and the church it led me to, I learned that the omnipresence of God includes the indwelling God spirit in every human being. We make the choice to recognize or ignore that always-available source of help. I finally understood the revelation in Genesis 1:26 that mankind was created in the image and likeness of God. For me, the image and likeness is in that indwelling presence.

How my life has changed since that awakening! Until we recognize that our spiritual needs are as important as our mental and physical requirements, we are missing out on the good life we could be having. It is true that mind affects the body and that bodily health affects the mind. Equally or perhaps even more important is the fact that the spirit aids both.

Now I consider myself to be a soul and a mind inhabiting a body. All three are a precious gift from God. He has entrusted me with their welfare and nourishment, and that is my lifetime assignment. Most important, and most gratifying, is tending to my spiritual health. Because being at one with God does wonders for the entire trinity of soul, mind, and body.

And the miracle of it is that we can *all* be at one with God at any time and in any place. We do not have to go to the Sea of Galilee. He is *always* with us. All we have to do is close our eyes and listen. In the glorious rhythm of His voice we will hear the music for our dance of life. And wherever we are and whatever our circumstances, we can partake in that dance with enthusiasm and joy!

DANCING LIGHTLY ON THE EDGES OF TIME
Every Day Is a New Beginning

Let your life lightly dance on the edges of
Time like dew on the tip of a leaf.

Rabindranath Tagore

Each of us is born with a God-given purpose
in life, a reason for existing. It is a purpose hidden
in our spiritual center, awaiting the awakening
that will inspire us to act upon it. Since it comes
from God, that purpose is never a purely selfish
one. It is also in some way, great or small, for
the good of other people too. For if we find peace
and happiness in living our lives to the fullest,
as God intends us to, surely the lives of those
we come in contact with will also be enhanced.
  When we are young, we are often so involved
with raising a family, making a living, and building a career that many of us cannot see beyond
our frantic day-to-day busyness. We think that
that is life. But it is only just a part of it. Life
is a series of new beginnings. It doesn't end when

the nest is empty, or when our working years wind down, or when we suddenly find ourselves without a partner and alone. It doesn't end — it *changes*. And every change is a challenge we should meet with hope and anticipation.

At the beginning of this century, the average life span in our country was just over forty-seven years. It is now close to eighty, and getting even longer as more of us learn to eat properly, exercise, and take good care of the body God gave us. For most of us, all those years can be active and productive. Though we may fear the specter of a nursing home, the most recent information from the Department of Health and Human Services says that, happily, it will not be a reality for the great majority of Americans: The proportion of all men and women between the ages of sixty-five and seventy-four *not* in a nursing home is 99%, and the proportion of men and women over eighty-five not in a nursing home is 85% for men and 75% for women!

Time is our enemy only if we choose to make it so. As we get older, we should look upon it not as something that is running out on us, but rather as something that is a precious gift from God. The dawn of each new day brings with it the opportunity for joy and fulfillment — if we will only listen to the prompting of our inner spirit and follow where it leads.

Recently a senior executive of a multibillion-dollar stockbrokerage retired at the age of fifty-nine. "I've done it long enough," he told reporters. "I'm still young enough to have another career in me." No matter what our age, we are *all* still young enough to have in us, if not another career, then another dream, another hope, another inspiration.

The choice of how to use each precious day is ours. Whatever we choose to do — work that needs attention, time outdoors tending the garden, a leisurely hour or two spent with friends or alone with a good book or creating a watercolor — we should know that doing our best will make it a good day. "This is a day the Lord has made; rejoice and be glad in it," we are told in Psalms 118:24.

Finding the right church or synagogue, one that brings us deeper spiritual understanding and strength, grows in importance as the years pass. In addition to bringing us inspiration for happier, more productive living, going to religious services regularly offers us opportunities for making friends — and even for extending our years of life.

As part of a scientific study of aging factors, a group of healthy, active centenarians were asked, "Do you feel that faith has helped you live longer?" The answer was a resounding *yes!*

As we get older, some of us may find ourselves confined financially or physically to areas close to home, or even to home itself. We should look upon that not as a limitation, but as a challenge. One evening not long ago, I switched on the TV in the middle of a newscast and saw a man in a wheelchair being interviewed. He was perhaps in his thirties and had obviously been badly injured. What he was saying moved me so profoundly that I wrote it down.

"The body was injured," he said, "but never the spirit — I turned it all over to God."

And from the light in his eyes and the lilt in his voice, it was apparent that his mind and spirit were in excellent health. With those two elements of the body-mind-spirit trio active and able to accept and even make light of physical limitations, that man will go on to build a new life, to dance to a lively beat even though he has to do it in a wheelchair. And since spiritual health is conducive to bodily health, perhaps someday he'll be able to leave that wheelchair and dance on his two feet again.

Life is a gift of endless possibilities, and we can find and enjoy the ones that are right for us if we will only open our eyes and our hearts. For even in a corner of our room, or in a wheelchair, or in our bed, we can, as the mystic poet William Blake wrote long ago:

> . . . see a world in a grain of sand
> And a heaven in a wild flower,
> Hold infinity in the palm of your hand
> And eternity in an hour.

What a powerhouse we have in our minds! If we emphasize the positive and do away with the negative, we can make our life dance joyful. All we have to do is let go of our doubts and let

God show us the way.

Every birthday should be an occasion of joy, a celebration of life, not a time to accept the outdated and erroneous notion that becoming sixty, seventy, eighty, or even ninety or one hundred puts a person in a sure decline. In May 1993, the legendary concert pianist Mieczyslaw Horszowski died just short of his 101st birthday. He had been giving concerts and delighting audiences with his music until shortly before his death, which is proof positive that decline will occur only if that is what we ourselves think will and must happen to us. Every age milestone will be exactly what we want it to be. We can see it as a marker we whirl by as we dance to the music of time, or as a boulder that is blocking our way. The choice is ours.

Of course there are problems we must deal with, and often they concern our physical health and strength. But if, like the man in the wheelchair, we keep our spirit strong, they will not be able to immobilize us. I treasure the story a friend told me about an old man who was asked how he could be so cheerful when he was burdened with so much trouble and had so few pleasures. "Well, it's like this," he said. "The Bible often says, 'And it came to pass.' It never says, 'It came to stay.'"

A sadness most of us who are blessed with mounting years must cope with is the death of friends and loved ones who share our personal history. What we must focus on then is not the sadness of the loss, but the joy we can derive from our memories, and the knowledge that those loved ones would want us to make the most of the time that is ours. A close friend, widowed a few years ago, told me she was going on a cruise soon. "That's what John told me I should do," she said. "He'd be glad I'm finally going to do it."

We can enhance the lives of younger friends and relatives if we use some of our time to write or record on tape our memories of earlier times and our observations about the changes we have seen in our lifetime. We can also ensure a breath of immortality here on earth for the friends and loved ones who are no longer with us by recording our memories of them, so that others may treasure them in their hearts as we do in ours.

And always, of course, there is the greatest joy and comfort of all — God. At *every* age, turning to God is the way toward a fulfilling, meaningful life. A deep sense of purpose, a goal of making our world a little better even in a small way is the road to satisfaction and true happiness. Only when we put God first can we truly hear His music and achieve a fuller life and inner peace.

Right now — this moment — take time out to close your eyes and listen to the music. We are here in life's big ballroom, and each of us, alone or with a partner, has a special dance to do, a dance that will make a difference in someone else's life and in our own — a positive difference, however small it may seem. God, the great dancing master, is telling us to listen to the music of our souls. He is sounding the beat that is right for each of us, the music to which we each may choreograph our life's dance. The first step out on the dance floor may seem difficult, but when we have found our beat, the dance will be filled with joy.

Listen to the music — and get up and join the dance!

SELECTED RESOURCES

The following is by no means a complete directory of organizations and publications that may be helpful to readers of this book, nor can the author and publisher take responsibility for replies to phone calls or letters. The information, phone numbers, and addresses are correct at the time of publication, but, like most things in this world, are subject to change. The listings concentrate only on recreational sources and are offered only as information that may be helpful, not as specific recommendations to individual readers.

General Organizations and Publications

As the number of Americans reaching their mature years has grown, so, too, has the number of organizations and publications devoted to their interests. You can find many simply by looking in your local telephone directory. In addition to the national groups mentioned below, you will find senior citizen groups in most communities and affiliated with most churches and synagogues.

AARP (Membership Center, P.O. Box 199, Long Beach, CA 90848-9983): The organization's name (American Association of Retired Persons) is misleading, because membership is open to people of 50 and up, regardless of retirement. Dues of $8 a year include the bimonthly magazine, *Modern Maturity*, the *AARP Bulletin*, and discounts, usually of 10%, at many motels and hotels. Services are also offered in supplemental health insurance, group travel, investments, auto and home insurance, and mail-order pharmaceuticals. AARP has about 4,000 local chapters and over 32 million members.

MATE OUTLOOK (6001 North Clark Street, Chicago, IL 60660. Phone: 1-800-336-6330): This association is for the 50+ group, and is affiliated with Sears. The annual membership fee of $9.95 includes the bimonthly magazine, *Mature Outlook: For Vibrant People Who Enjoy Life*, and newsletter; 10% discount coupons for purchases of $20 or more at any Sears store; special discounts at Sears optical departments; and, with some restrictions, a 50% discount at "ITC50" listed hotels, motels, and resorts. Special services similar to AARP's are also available.

NEW CHOICES FOR RETIREMENT LIVING (P.O. Box 1945, Marion, OH 43305-1945): Published ten months a year, this quality magazine is of general interest to the mature, retired or otherwise. Its wide variety of articles and columns are written from a positive viewpoint and slanted toward the 50+ group.

Service Organizations

When we help others, we help ourselves through the pleasure of doing something useful and the friendships we make. You can find many local volunteer organizations listed in your phone book under *Volunteer*. Or call your church or synagogue, favorite charity, local hospital, schools, libraries, museums, animal shelters, and community organizations. Your offer of help is sure to be welcomed! Those with particular business skills may want to contact:

SCORE (409 Third Street, SW, Suite 5900, Washington, DC 20024): Established in 1964 by the Small Business Administration to utilize the talents of newly retired persons, the Service Corps of Retired Executives Association is not limited to retirees. Its counselors assist small-business operators upon request, counseling them without charge.

Service, Learning, & Travel Combined

Some organizations combine volunteer service with learning and travel, enabling us to double and even triple our pleasure as we help others. Here are a few:

ELDERHOSTEL (75 Federal Street, Boston, MA 02110): Self-described as "an educational adventure," Elderhostel is devoted to both learning and service experiences. Membership is open to those 60 and over and to spouses and companions of 50+. (Detailed information begins on page 129.) Fees include registration, meals, and room. Members provide their own travel. Those interested in volunteer programs may choose among several that are affiliated with Elderhostel, such as Global Volunteers, Oceanic Society Expeditions, and the domestically popular Habitat for Humanity. If you write for information, specify which catalogs you want: United States and Canada, international, or both.

OUTWARD BOUND USA (Department 93A, Route 2, Box 280, Garrison, NY 10524-9757. Phone: 1-800-243-8520): Through its adventure-based courses, this organization strives to "inspire self-esteem, concern for others, and care for the environment." (See also pp. 143–4.) Some courses have age restrictions, all are given in small groups, and safety is a major priority. Outdoor experience is not necessarily required, but good health and a willingness to try new experiences are.

SIERRA CLUB (730 Polk Street, San Francisco, CA 94109. Phone: 415-776-2211): Devoted to conservation and the environment, the club has membership fees that range from $15 for seniors on upward. Membership includes a subscription to *Sierra* magazine and eligibility to apply for inclusion in the club's outings and vacations, which are devoted to domestic and foreign service and exploration. There is a minimum age for many expeditions. Walking and backpacking are often involved, and good physical health is a requirement at any age.

Education for the Fun of It

Life is an ongoing learning experience, and we are surrounded by opportunities to expand our knowledge both inside and outside of our homes. And isn't it nice that we can have all the pleasure of learning whatever we want at whatever pace we choose — with none of the pain of examinations! Elderhostel and other groups that offer a combination of learning and travel are listed above, but there are many learning resources close at hand:

AARP MINICOURSES: These are offered to groups of seniors. For more information write: AARP Fulfillment, P.O. Box 2400, Long Beach, CA 90801. Ask for the Minicourse Order Form (D1618).

ADULT EDUCATION: Almost every college and many high schools offer the general public not-for-credit courses on a wide range of subjects. For information, call the colleges and high schools in your area.

LIBRARIES: Your local library offers you a wealth of free information, but if you think that information is available only in books, take another look! Many libraries now have video and audio cassette collections too. You can learn to speak a foreign language by listening to tapes or travel to another country via video. And many libraries have book-discussion clubs, readings, talks, and slide lectures. Libraries have large-print books for patrons with vision problems, and, of course, for the blind and handicapped there are Talking Books and books in Braille. For information about the Talking Books program, telephone 1-800-424-8567. If you are handicapped and cannot leave your home, call your local library and ask if they have a Bookmobile or offer some other service that will bring materials to your home.

Crafts, Hobbies, Sports, & Games

There are so many occupations with which we can fill the hours! Entire books have been devoted to a single craft, hobby, sport, or game. All you have to do is choose one — and go to the library to find out all about it. If it's cooking or sewing, you may even find that your library has a pattern and recipe exchange! If you want to join a club or association devoted to your special interest, ask to see the Encyclopedia of Associations in the research department. Published by Gale Research, this encyclopedia lists thousands of clubs and organizations, from those associated with trade and business interests, through those devoted to hobbies, crafts, ethnic and religious interests, and even fan clubs! A very abbreviated sampling of associations follows:
AMERICAN CRAFTS COUNCIL (72 Spring

Street, New York, NY 10012. Phone: 212-274-0630) is an umbrella group that can provide you with information about crafts and many hobbies.

ELDER CRAFTSMEN (135 East 65th Street, New York, NY 10021. Phone: 212-861-5260) is a nonprofit organization that advises seniors in the making and selling of handcrafts. For information, call or send $1 and a stamped, self-addressed envelope to the above address.

COMPUTERS: For those who love computing, there's **Senior Net** (399 Arguello Boulevard, San Francisco, CA 94118. Phone: 415-750-5030), a nonprofit group that offers seniors newsletters, learning centers, tutorials, the opportunity to network, and other computer privileges. Membership is $25 a year. Call or write for an information packet.

GAMES: If you enjoy playing cards and board games, you should get in touch with your local senior center and the recreation division of your department of parks. Many of them have clubs, and some even organize tournaments. Both the **U.S. Chess Federation** (186 Route 9W, New Windsor, NY 12553. Phone: 914-562-8350) and the **American Contract Bridge League** (P.O. Box 161192, Memphis, TN 38186. Phone: 901-332-5586) offer members benefits that extend far beyond learning and playing the games.

GARDENING: Cultivate friendships as well as roses. For information on garden clubs in your state, contact the **National Council of State Garden Clubs**, 4401 Magnolia Avenue, St. Louis,

MO 63110 (Phone: 314-776-7574). Or, if you have no backyard or are housebound, you can bring a garden indoors. The **Indoor Gardening Society of America** (944 South Munroe Road, Tallmadge, OH 44278) has clubs throughout the country. Membership fee of $19.95 includes a subscription to *Houseplant* magazine, round robins, and the chance to meet with and exchange ideas with other enthusiasts. For information, write to Sharon Zentz, Membership Secretary.

GENEALOGY: This is one of the fastest growing hobbies in the country. For information on how to trace your roots, write to the **National Archives Trust Fund Board**, Box 129, the National Archives & Records Administration, Washington, DC 20408.

SPORTS: Every sport you can think of, from archery through walking, has at least one national association that can put you in touch with local clubs and activities in your area. For information, check your phone book and the *Encyclopedia of Associations* at your library.

STAMP COLLECTING: This is a popular hobby that many people begin in childhood and never lose interest in. If you want to start a collection or get information about the one you have, get in touch with the **American Philatelic Society**, P.O. Box 8000, State College, PA 16803.

Travel Publications & Planning Aids

For people 50 and over, there are many fine

senior travel tours available, and often at quite moderate rates. Check with your travel agent for more information about them. Also, whatever your favorite mode of travel — train, ship, bus, or airplane — don't forget to ask if senior rates are available!

AMTRAK offers, through its Great American Vacations program, over 90 trips, ranging from self-guided to fully escorted tours. Air-rail and rail-sail combinations are also available. For information see your travel agent or call 1-800-321-8684.

FORSYTH TRAVEL LIBRARY (9154 West 57th Street, P.O. Box 2975, Shawnee Mission, KS 66201-1375) specializes in European rail travel and offers information on passes. You can purchase the type you need through them prior to your trip. Forsyth also sells guidebooks and maps. Write for a catalog.

FREIGHTER WORLD CRUISES (180 South Lake #335, Pasadena, CA 91101. Phone: 818-449-3106) is a twice-monthly newsletter about passenger services on freighters. A one-year subscription is $33.

GREAT CANADIAN RAILTOUR COMPANY, LTD., conducts rail-based tour packages through the Rockies from Vancouver to Jasper, Banff, and Calgary. It also has combination train and bus tours. For a brochure, call 1-800-665-7245.

THE INTERNATIONAL RAILWAY TRAVELER (Subscription Services, Department IRT, P.O. Box 3000, Denville, NJ 07834-9867) is a bimonthly publication specializing in railway travel outside the U.S. A one-year subscription is $39.95.

NATIONAL PARKS: Our national parks are the most beautiful in the world, and many tours of them are available. Check with your travel agent and Amtrak, or call 1-800-365-2267. Seniors 62 and older may obtain free Golden Age passports from the National Park Service at any federal park or monument that charges a fee. The passports provide free admission and also 50% off some other fees and services.

SAGA INTERNATIONAL HOLIDAYS, LTD. (222 Berkeley Street, Boston, MA 02116-9489. Phone: 1-800-343-0273), is a worldwide travel agency that specializes in trips for travelers 60 and over (companions 50+). The package price includes air fare to and from a major city on regularly scheduled flights; accommodations and meals as specified; medical, flight, and baggage insurance; transportation to and from hotels; luggage handling; admissions to listed excursion features; guide services; and visas if needed. A Saga representative meets travelers on arrival and is available at most times.

TRAVLTIPS (P.O. Box 188, Flushing, NY 11358. Phone: 1-800-872-8584) is a magazine devoted to the interests of freighter passengers. Since freighter-passenger lines have diminished, *TravLtips* also offers discounts on selected expeditions and unusual cruises. Membership of $30 a year includes the bimonthly magazine and frequent special mailings.

DATE			